TESTIMONIALS
REACTIONS FROM READERS

"Here is a book, the writing of which has clearly played a key role in the author's long, and at times bedeviled, path toward recovery from childhood sexual abuse, that serves as an 'intervention' bringing hope, inspiration and guidance for others who have been similarly victimized. It is, in fact, a story that will resonate with anyone whose life has become unhinged by a traumatic event that has left them feeling alone, isolated from the world around them, yet fearing the consequences from sharing their 'secret' and feelings with others."

—W. H., VP, Major Transportation Company/Retired

"I had to take a few days 'off' to digest and internalize what I'd read … you and I have so many parallels; your clarity of vision on those behaviors and your objective evaluation, especially the tone of self-forgiveness, were a tremendous boon for me. In summary, I enjoyed every moment of my time with you in your journey. You truly have an amazingly important story to tell!

"So much of your story resonates quite deeply with me … I acted out in a very similar fashion, and it has been startling to read that so much of what you felt and did parallels my own journey!"

—A. O., Executive, Health Association/Retired

"Compelling; very well written."

—M. H., Director, Religious Education

"The author is 'extremely courageous,' but I am 'so sorry that she suffered' as she did. Her story 'made me think that I could use another go through the Hoffman Institute to get to the deeper layers.'

"Thank God for her husband Jamie's love for her …"

—**D. K., Policy Analyst**

"I have had time to read your brutally honest book. I am awed by the devotion you and Jamie have for each other, as well as the supportive strengths you share in difficult, even devastating times.

"Two things stand out for me: The first is the mettle you demonstrate in your willingness to be fearless in your self-examination and attempts to know, understand, and accept yourself. Such a daunting task for any of us, but particularly so for someone emerging from abuse and looking to move beyond mere survival to thriving and living her life with rich texture and depth and honesty. Surely you know that few of us can make that transition, but you did, and with writing about your journey, you make it possible for others to travel a similar path.

"The second part that hits me with an emotional wallop is that perhaps if the almost unspeakable tragedy of Jeffrey's death had not happened, you might not have been spurred to seek relief from a pain to which you had almost become unconscious, that with his death, he gave you and Jamie the opportunity to find new life.

"Thank you for sharing your story and journey with me. I salute you and Jamie and the love and courage you have shared these many years. Sending affection and wishing you peace."

—**J. B., Family Therapist**

Demons
Hidden
Within

*Lifelong Impact of Child
Sexual Abuse*

Susan Montgomery

Robert D. Reed Publishers • Bandon, OR

Robert D. Reed Publishers
P.O. Box 1992
Bandon, OR 97411
Phone: 541-347-9882; Fax: -9883
E-mail: 4bobreed@msn.com
Website: www.rdrpublishers.com

Editors: Mary Ann Raemisch and Cleone Lyvonne Reed
Designer: Amy Cole
Cover: Jamie Vail and Cleone Lyvonne Reed

Softcover ISBN: 978-1-63821-512-7
EBook ISBN: 978-1-63821-514-1
Library of Congress Number: 2021935667

Designed and Printed in the United States of America

Nothing contained in this book is or should be considered or used as a substitute for professional medical or mental health advice, diagnosis, or treatment. You should seek the advice of your physician or other qualified health professional with any questions you may have regarding a medical or mental health condition.

DEDICATION

This book is dedicated to our son Jeffrey,
who was a delight while he lived, and who, in death,
devastated me until I began the difficult task of healing,
both from his death and from the early trauma I suffered.

TABLE OF CONTENTS

ACKNOWLEDGMENTS

As I journeyed through life working through several traumas, I eventually learned I needed the help of others. I discovered I simply could not handle my issues by myself.

My wise and patient psychotherapist for ten years, Judith Halpern, literally saved my life. And a decade later, Linda Killian provided essential therapeutic support at a time of need. I especially appreciate both Linda and my very good friend, Fran Gress, for getting me started on writing my memoir.

As in my life, the creation of this book required the assistance of others. First, and foremost, was the help given by my loving companion of over 60 years, my husband Jamie. He continually guided me through the intricacies of MS Word® as well as the numerous challenges involved in having my written word appear in print.

In her professional and insightful edit of the book, Mary Ann Raemisch proved her worth again and again. And to our benefit, she stayed with me, despite my intransigence.

Support for the book also came from several readers who shared their heartfelt reactions: I particularly want to thank Ann Walker, Amy Patterson O'Keefe, and Veronica Swain Kunz for their untiring insights and expert critique, which have caused the manuscript to grow into its present form.

Finally, through all the years I have had the unwavering support of my two lovely daughters, Maria and Rachel, who have always supplied me with encouraging warm words and hugs when I needed them most.

NOTE TO READERS

The events concerning my life I describe here are true; however, several names and places have been changed in order to provide a modicum of privacy to those mentioned.

In the interest of keeping this memoir historically accurate, I have had access to almost 300 letters I wrote to my future husband Jamie during the early years of our friendship as well as fifteen detailed journals I wrote off and on during our life together.

During my life, I suffered from two heart-wrenching traumas—childhood sexual abuse and a family tragedy. The family issue sent me into therapy where I worked through both of the traumas emotionally. My therapist also attempted to address my behavioral issues but with limited success.

It was only when I began planning this book I decided I could not honestly write about my life or my behavior unless I understood why it was noticeably unhealthy. Since I had no answers, I began reading extensively, concurrent with conducting research online. What I discovered is that my behavior was unconsciously caused by the unresolved sexual abuse. I have included these citations in my story, as I realized they were key to understanding my actions.

The list of references is by no means complete, but I feel it is sufficiently representative for my purposes.

FOREWORD

On one level this is a tale about the impact of sexual abuse and healing from it. On another level it is a love story which started when I told my teenage boyfriend about the abuse, and he accepted me anyway, thus beginning our relationship of more than sixty-eight years. The sexual abuse I experienced almost derailed me; much later my husband and I suffered the devastating loss of our son. Ultimately, then, this is the story of healing from the terrible traumas, which life threw at us.

Our son's suicide was devastating; living through the grief, despair, guilt, anger, and sadness which resulted from the tragedy engulfed me. I could easily fill another book with this story, but I have chosen here to focus particularly on the sexual abuse in order to help break the silence surrounding the issue.

It is a story which requires telling, written in support of the millions who have been sexually abused as children. This is not an exaggeration; a survey of over 17,000 adult members of a health maintenance organization (HMO) revealed that approximately 25% of women and 7–8% of men reported being sexually abused as children.[1] This book is written particularly for all survivors, as well as the victims of other traumas, and also for the therapists who work with them. It is my purpose *to try to help these survivors, through my experience, recognize the long-reaching, damaging effects abuse can play in their lives, although the connection or link may not be perceived at the time.*

This has been an emotionally difficult book to write because it has forced me to look back at some painful memories of the incest and of my ensuing aberrant behavior. I have learned, as countless other survivors have discovered, that *child sexual abuse can unconsciously sabotage the survivor's life without some type of intervention.*

After I experienced the trauma of my teenage son's suicide in 1985, I finally started working with a psychotherapist, which was the beginning

3

of understanding the root cause of my unhealthy behavior was the sexual abuse I experienced in my childhood. Although I never forgot what had happened to me, I thought I could be free of the effects of the sexual trauma by simply putting it away, out of my thoughts. But instead of helping, the psychic energy required to bury the abuse prevented me from living consciously—and it was living *unconsciously* which made me especially vulnerable to many troublesome behaviors.

I know from experience we who were sexually abused as children tend not to reveal the trauma we experienced; but as renowned psychiatrist Bessel van der Kolk observed, it is "… secrets like these [which] become inner toxins—realities that [one] is not allowed to acknowledge to [oneself] or others but nevertheless become the template of [one's] life."[2] Sadly, this template refers to the unhealthy behavior of mine which seemed (to others) to be completely pointless, senseless, and incomprehensible. In one single, remarkable phrase which characterizes much of my life, he further notes that survivors "… with these histories [of abuse] rarely make the connection between what happened to them long ago and how they currently feel and behave."[3]

Therapy was a godsend for me, a lifesaver, as I tackled first our son's death, and then the sexual abuse. Thus, 1985 became a turning point when therapy started me on the long, tortuous road eventually leading to healing. It was a slow process, as there were many coping behaviors from the past I had to unlearn and attitudes I needed to change. I remember, for instance, I had learned to trust myself alone at the time of the abuse, only to discover when my son died I needed other people, sometimes desperately.

I would be less than honest if I left you with the impression that my life, even in the early days, was troubled by the incest to the point it prevented me from finding anything of value or goodness in it. In my memoir, I have identified much which was wonderful, such as my husband, children, and special friends. My husband is likely the most important of these, as I met him when I was young; and his love and care helped offset some of the effects of the abuse which was happening at home.

This is intended to be a message of hope to survivors. I am a survivor; I am living a psychologically healthy and happy life today because I chose, during a dark time of my adult life, to seek help, enabling me to begin healing from the abuse.

Erin Carpenter, a psychotherapist and trauma specialist, notes that the job in healing is to *"weave the [trauma] into the larger narrative of the survivor's life,"*[4] which is the ultimate goal of this process. A University of Washington professor, Riki Thompson, has observed that *"child sexual abuse survivors have capitalized on the genre of narrative in order to heal their own emotional wounds as well as to create a public discourse, which is aimed at ending the cycle of child sexual abuse…"*[5]

And it is because I *have* now healed I wish to share this story with you. As Karen Duncan, a marriage and family therapist says, *"Sharing with other women who have lived through this trauma and healed can facilitate an exchange of hope among women."*[6]

1 THE EARLY YEARS

1

FAST FORWARD
TO THE PAST

"For some [abused children], family life was chaotic."[7]

Picture a distressing scene in a child's darkened bedroom in a modest home in Schenectady, New York, during the mid-1940s. Huddled under the bed, my brother, sister, and I were trembling in fear. We were very young, too young to make sense of what was happening. We felt vulnerable and in desperate need of protection. Somewhere outside the bedroom our parents were yelling violently, threatening one another. Were these the same parents who took care of us? We were shaking in fear and clung to one another for safety. I remember being afraid our parents would kill each other and us in the crossfire.

How often were we forced to seek safety under the bed?

In one of her books, author Karen Duncan talks about the dynamics in troubled families. The parents exhibit "… absolute power and control over children …;" they establish rules, which are "… arbitrary and rigid …" There is also a general disrespect for the children, who are told they should be "… seen but not heard …" Furthermore, there are such "… inconsistencies and contradictions …" in an abusive family, which produce such a sense of "chaos and uncertainty in turn, [it can] cause a great deal of emotional instability within the family."[8]

Duncan's description mimics my childhood growing up in my family.

My background was not exceptional. I was born shortly before the U.S. entry into WWII. My family lived in a middle-class neighborhood in upstate New York. Ours was the American family modeled after TV's Ozzie and Harriet. On the surface, we lived the dream, but it didn't go any deeper! I was happy at school and with my friends, but at home my parents were always fighting. It was frightening. We children were more comfortable being out of the house. Despite the chaos, my mother was busy trying to figure out how to manage the family. She did jump in to protect my sister sometimes, but she didn't realize I needed help too. She saw my father seemed to get along with me better than anybody else in the family. She thought, therefore, I was safer than my siblings; she didn't realize it also made me more vulnerable.

Our family dynamic actively discouraged family members from feeling close. The tension kept laughter at bay; luckily my sister and I had each other.

Meeting on a blind date, my parents' introduction was unusual. Mother worked very hard to give my father a rosy impression of her. She had a friend, who came over with her tiny baby and whipped up a delicious meal. Then she sent her friend away. When my dad arrived, my mother put on a show demonstrating her expertise with babies and her equally amazing skills in the kitchen as well. When my dad realized the lengths she had gone to in order to impress him, he was taken with her. They were married six months later. My mother used to tell us how she sat in a rocking chair the morning of her wedding and announced she was not going to get married. I sometimes think her instinct to avoid marriage—or avoid marriage to my father specifically—may have been entirely reasonable.

Earlier in life she had been a very successful assistant buyer for one of the big department stores in New York City and loved it! Perhaps she was meant to be a business woman; maybe this was where her talent, ability, and interest really lay.

The Depression proved to be a harsh reality for my father. He graduated from Yale with an engineering degree and spent his honeymoon writing letters for jobs. He was hired by a company in Philadelphia to sell specialty oils, which hardly made use of his education. After a year at the home base, his territory was moved to Schenectady.

When I was four, my maternal grandmother had arranged to rent a cottage for herself in St. Petersburg, Florida, for three months; but when the time came, she wasn't up to making the trip. My mom leaped at the chance to take her place. She loved to jump in the car and go off on adventures, not letting her three children stop her either! There is part of me which has to admire my mother for her courage, her spirit of adventure, and her spunk!

She drove us children from upstate New York to St. Petersburg, Florida. There were no interstates, and the roads we drove on were slow. Our car didn't have power steering or turn signals. We drove for three days and stopped only for meals and sleep.

The bungalow in St. Petersburg was very modest. It was all on one floor with a screened-in porch. We liked it immediately. The weather was warm, and we were near the ocean. Our time there was tranquil. My father wasn't with us, which made my mother seem far less stressed and anxious. I don't remember her even raising her voice or getting angry; she seemed happy. I think our behavior and our demeanor reflected my mother's, which meant, for these three months at least, it really was a very peaceful time.

When we arrived back home, my father, with my mother's approval, had sold our house, but we couldn't move into our new place yet. My brother, sister, and I all came down with measles. Since we couldn't stay in a hotel, our parents came up with an unusual solution—we were admitted to a local hospital until we were well again.

Sloane was a troublemaker, even in the hospital. He climbed out of bed for fun one day, and when the nurse came into the room, he hid in the wastebasket. Ann and I watched, full of suspense, but the nurse never even noticed he wasn't in his bed. We had a good laugh afterward.

A real-life respite from our parents' combative quarrels occurred when my mother hired Catherine, a lovely, middle-aged lady, to take care of us. She quickly became a favorite of my brother, sister, and mine. Our parents could be tired and cross, but she was always even tempered, always caring. She was a surrogate mother to us, especially my sister. Catherine would have done anything in her power on our behalf. She was one of the brightest spots in our childhood.

Unfortunately our parents' fights were frequent. One time we kids had gone to a Saturday matinee at the local movie theater when the manager's voice on the loudspeaker reprimanded some kids for being rowdy. "The next troublemakers will be thrown out of the theater," he added. Maybe five minutes later we heard our names being called and started wondering what we had done. But it was only our mother collecting us, so we could accompany her as she drove to Buffalo. This was where her lawyer lived. After a fight with our father, her intention was to see the lawyer about a divorce. We would then drive 90 miles to Utica, where we

would have dinner and spend the night. The next day, she would have calmed down, and we would invariably turn around and drive home. I am not certain how many times this occurred, but we never made it past Utica.

How often did my parents fight? Did it happen often enough to make us inured to them?

I remember a particular time when we kids were unfortunately home to hear it all. Our parents were upstairs, yelling and screaming, while we were downstairs, trying to distract ourselves any way we could. They both had violent tempers, and we were well aware of the difference in their sizes. This put my mother at a real disadvantage, and we worried she could be hurt. When the fight was over and my father had left,

13

I crept up the stairs to see how my mother was. She was sitting in her rocking chair, rocking. I asked her if she was all right. She was somber but assured me she was. Often she would end up with a black eye and tell people she had run into a door. I doubt she ever fooled anybody.

But the conflict exhibited by my parents was not limited to the two of them. No, my mom did not get along with her mother-in-law either. When my grandmother came to visit us, my mother would leave and stay with a friend for the duration of the visit. Grandma took advantage of my mom's absence. When my brother Sloane was five, my sister Ann was three, and I was four, we still hadn't been baptized in the Episcopal Church because my maternal grandmother in Buffalo was ill. My mother wanted to wait for her to be well enough to come for the ceremony.

During one of my grandmother's visits, she and my father arranged with a local minister to have the three of us baptized in a private ceremony without my mother! We were all much too young to say, "Stop! Wait for our mother! She needs to be here!" I think my brother and I knew, though, that this was not right, but we had no power, no voice. When my mother came home and found out, she was enraged! I can only imagine her fury at being robbed of her children's baptism! It was an intentional and cruel insult to her.

Another time, a few years later, my sister and I were visiting our grandma. Our hair back then had these beautiful shoulder-length ringlets my mother loved. My grandmother didn't. She did not want to fool with our hair, washing and combing it every day; her solution was to take us to a barbershop, where they cut the curls off and shingled the back. There were no curls left and little hair. When we drove home and my mother saw us, she wept.

But we tried to maintain a sense of normalcy in our lives. When I was in first grade, we kids would travel home at lunchtime every day, and Catherine would give us big hugs and plates full of good food before sending us back to school. Afterwards, she would be there to ask about our days.

Our house was close enough to the school to walk, and my best friend lived just a block away. Jeannie and I were in the same class and did everything together, like sleepovers, dance classes, and Girl Scout Camp in the summers.

Over time I started having frequent nightmares. The details are fuzzy, but I know my best friend Jeannie's father was always the villain. I used to puzzle over these dreams. Because I knew Jeannie's dad a little and liked him, I could not figure out why he would be evil in my dreams.

I wondered if he may have been a stand-in for my father, maybe because it was safer, or more acceptable, to have scary dreams about my friend's father than about my own.

In the meantime, my mother inherited money from her mother, enabling her to escape at times from home and responsibility. Catherine would be there to take care of us children, which allowed my mom, in good conscience, to spend afternoons with her friends, eating out, playing bridge, and drinking. The drinking started slowly but gradually became a daily habit, which got worse as we children were growing up. There were many times when she went to bed drunk.

It was only much later I realized she drank to cope with her unhappy marriage. My father had convinced her there had never been a divorce in the family, which he did intentionally to keep her from using this option.

2

SHATTERED

"The historical consensus on father-daughter incest during the post-WWII years in the U.S. is that it was fully and effectively denied by social workers, courts of law, criminologists, psychoanalysts, social scientists, and ultimately the public at large."[9]

"Sometimes the mother's failure to act as a restraining agent is a simple matter of her not being present in the home when the incestuous situation is developing."[10]

It was a warm evening during the summer, shortly after my family had moved to Scotia, New York, a suburb of Schenectady. I was eleven. On August 14, 1952, my brother Sloane and my sister Ann had left on a trip with my mom. She was taking them to Sandusky, Ohio, to her cousin's funeral. They were going to stop and see the house where her grandmother had lived.

The plan was for my father to drive me to Atlantic City the next day, where we would spend a few days with my paternal grandmother.

I don't know how my parents made the decision as to which child would go where. I do remember, though, my position in the family was as "Daddy's little girl." This may have been the key. I felt special; maybe he made me feel special. I was happy when I could spend time with my father. I think now about how innocent I was then and how unable to predict what it would mean to be "special."

Everything that day was fine. Then at night, we headed to bed and he asked, "How would you like to sleep with me?" We were standing in the hall between my parents' bedrooms, which were separate. While he had twin beds in his room, she had a double bed. I wasn't happy about the idea of not sleeping in my own room, but I answered in the affirmative. Then he said, "We'll sleep in your mother's room." My heart sank. I thought we would sleep in the twin beds. Deep down, I knew I did not want to sleep in bed with him. I said nothing to my father, but it seemed significant I opposed this idea, even before anything happened.

My reaction then has made me wonder if other unsavory things had happened before this particular night. I didn't remember anything else, but I am aware memories can be repressed.

I didn't know how to say no gracefully without hurting my dad's feelings. I worried about him instead of myself. I have always asked myself why I didn't tell him no. Why didn't I resist? My sister would have. But I was not my sister. Furthermore, I seem to have been worrying about him, even though he was the parent and should have been taking care of me.

What happened next is forever etched in my memory. We got in bed, and in the dark, my father pulled off his pajama bottoms. I knew exactly what he was doing because he told me. I was lying on my back in the bed, and he lifted up my nightgown. My heart stopped as I held my breath. I still remember the exact words he said.

"As part of your education, I am going to demonstrate something you need to avoid with a man. I am going to show you what it feels like when a man's sex organ touches you." Then he lowered himself on top of me, his penis touching my vaginal lips. I must have been sensitive there because I jumped as he touched me. He lay back down and remarked as he did, "I didn't realize you would be that tender."

I remember reading a quote from clinical psychologist and author Karin Meiselman, who perfectly described the false basis often used by dads—like my father—to [justify] acts of incest: *Some daughters are given a 'sex education' rationale which is the most common single deceptive technique reported in the literature.*"[11]

I was relieved he stopped before penetrating me. I started to breathe easier but realized suddenly the ordeal wasn't over. My father was back in his pajama bottoms, but then he turned on a bright overhead light and pulled out a small, handheld mirror. He had me sit up and then pulled up my nightgown again. Using the mirror, he pointed out the two holes in my vulva—the urethra for the discharge of urine and the other opening, the vagina, for sex. I was mortified and wanted to disappear, to escape somehow from the bedroom. My brain went numb. I had this feeling I had died deep inside. I could not come to grips with the shock of what he had done. As an eleven-year-old, I couldn't handle the emotions. Instinctively, I divorced myself from my feelings in order to survive.

I knew my father had betrayed my trust badly enough I would never feel the same about him again. I would never be comfortable alone with him. The worst was my awareness that his actions had changed me irrevocably. I suddenly understood the world was not a safe place—there had been nobody to help me when I desperately needed protection. I closed up inside, feeling completely alone. Damaged as I was, I knew I must somehow protect myself. I felt terribly hurt, locked in a world of secrecy.

After this, my father warmed milk for us, and we went to sleep. I did sleep too. Perhaps I was hoping to escape the memory; but when I woke in the morning, the nightmare was still with me. Sleep didn't cure the hurt or erase my feelings. The abuse had deeply scarred my brain.

The next day my father acted like nothing had happened, while I was dying inside. After breakfast he took me to stay with Catherine for a few hours while he finished his work. I have no memory of the morning or how I got through it. I believe I was numb. I do remember deciding I could not tell Catherine my secret. I loved and trusted her, but she would undoubtedly report it to my mother. My mom would either not believe Catherine or discharge her because the secret unleashed would be a threat to the standing of my family in the community. Instinctively I knew I did not want to lose Catherine.

I decided not to tell my mother either. I could not figure out what she would do with the information, but I was afraid the knowledge—and her reaction—might cause our family to be destroyed. It was this fear of the consequences of disclosure, which helped create my sense of powerlessness—a condition I carried into my adult life. In fact, researchers Finkelhor and Browne describe powerlessness to be one of the four principle factors characterizing the impact of child sexual abuse.[12]

Moreover, I had "this forlorn internal sense of there being nobody I could turn to and nothing I could do to stop the abuse. I really was powerless."[13]

My husband, Jamie, told me my depiction of being really alone to deal with the abuse strikes a chord. People today might have difficulty relating to my situation back in the early fifties. If I had gone to seek help, I most likely would not have been believed.

I suffered the horror and the shame alone and in silence for a very long time. This was my secret to bury deep, away from my awareness, because I did not feel comfortable talking about it or even thinking about it.

When my father and I left for the long drive from the Schenectady area to my grandmother's in New Jersey, just the two of us, it was torturous for me. I no longer trusted this man I called Dad. I felt extremely anxious alone in the car with him. There was a map open on the front seat of the car, and to control my thoughts and my anxiety, I silently read what was printed on the sides of the map over and over: "Drive carefully. The life you save may be your own," and, "You can be dead right also." Somehow the repetitive chanting worked, and I not only made it safely through the trip, but I was fairly successful at blocking thoughts of the abuse as well. I had, in essence, learned not to think about dangerous things, although I don't believe I was fully conscious of this at the time. The ability to put problems away and not think about them probably served me well at age eleven. But the psychological literature cautions that if the behavior persists into adulthood, this skewed habit of not thinking about important issues could become maladaptive and lead to some very dire consequences.

Since this time, I have often thought of our car ride. I not only learned to stop thinking, but it was the start of my obsessive-compulsive behavior as well. I believe it was also the beginning of my depression, although I remember it more as feeling numb or dead inside. I was in junior high, and I have very few memories of my subsequent time there.

Another strange story about my father and me never made sense to me. It happened, I believe, shortly before the abuse, and I have always wondered if it was significant.

He and I were alone on one of the islands at Lake George. I don't have any idea why we were there or where the rest of my family was. We'd gotten to the island by boat; we must have been walking back to it when my father, out of the blue, spied an unidentified red berry growing on a bush. He picked it off, put it in his mouth, and said, "I wonder if it's poisonous." I couldn't figure out why he would eat something toxic, but I remember thinking if he was going to do this, then I would also. And since I was walking behind him, he didn't see me when I picked off a berry and ate it. Is this because I identified with him?

Besides, I've never figured out if he was really unsure about the berry, or if he wanted to make himself important in my eyes.

I have no idea what actually happened on the island before my father ate the berry, but I suspect this was when something untoward could have happened, something, which convinced me later I did not want to sleep with him. He must have done something causing me to stop trusting him, but I don't remember what it was.

There seem to be quite a few unanswered questions like the legal one. The abuse was clearly morally wrong as well as being against the law. But think about a legal case, which would have required me to publicly accuse my father in court. This would have been emotionally exhausting for me as well as quite possibly destroying my family.

In addition, I don't believe it would have helped me to forget the horror of the night nor cured the numbness I felt afterward. I had forever lost the comfortable, loving relationship I used to have with my father.

At this point, I had no idea how the effects of the sexual abuse might play out in my life.

3

SUMMERS

*"Lake George [NY] is without comparison,
the most beautiful water I ever saw."*[14]

I buried the abuse, thinking I could perhaps forget the experience, and thus be able to enjoy the good times ahead. My family was extremely fortunate to be able to spend our summers at Lake George, New York, where we had some of our happiest times. The water was pure then; in fact, people simply drew water from the lake for drinking. This has changed now.

At one point, my parents found a small cabin for sale on the lake's west side, north of Lake George Village. It wasn't actually on the lake. My father wouldn't buy a place on the water until we could all swim. The cabin was in a ravine; a stream ran under a corner of the porch. There was no easy access over the stream, resulting in my father and my friend Jeannie's father building a bridge for us to walk on. There was running water in the kitchen; and since there was no bathroom, we had to use an outdoor latrine. I loved this cabin and adored going to sleep to the sound of the babbling brook.

In 1952, when we could all swim, my parents purchased a cottage on the water on the east side of the lake, which was more residential than the commercial west side. We stayed at the lake all summer, but my mother was only there during the week and my father on the weekends.

When we moved to our new cottage, there were kids close to our age nearby, giving us instant playmates. There was a boy named James next door, but everybody called him Jamie. I met him the same summer I was sexually abused, literally just a few weeks before it happened. I wonder sometimes if he was sent to me to take care of me. At least I like to think that's true.

Next to Jamie lived John, who had just come to this country from Germany and didn't speak any English at the time; and then there was Roberta, who was a bit of a tomboy. With my sister Ann and me, there were five of us; and we were together constantly. My brother was a water ski instructor at a "Y" camp nearby and was never with us.

On nice days, we were always in the water. We made up our own water game we called the Flipper game, which involved one person wearing flippers and swimming underwater, and the others trying to get the flippers off him or her. In retrospect, this was a way to have physical contact with the opposite sex.

When we tired of this, we took a canoe out in the bay and tipped it over; then we swam under the edge of the canoe and popped up in the air space underneath, where we could talk to one another.

Since John's family had a boathouse, four of us kids decided one morning we were going to dive into the water from the boathouse roof. It was about eight or nine feet high. We all dove in successfully except Ann, who changed her mind at the last possible moment and landed feet first on the dock. I was glad she hadn't landed head first, but it must have hurt.

Jamie's dock was the center point of all of our fun. His family was very musical. They loved to sing, and Jamie's brother-in-law played the accordion. On Saturday evenings they sometimes gathered on the dock to sing; and my father, Ann, and I would join them, as well as the neighbors from the other side. There would be a whole group of us together on the dock, singing our hearts out, and people in boats on the water came by and stopped, with their navigation lights on, to hear the music. It was great fun, and again, there was a wonderful sense of community emanating from the group of us friends and neighbors, singing and making music together. Being in a community has always made me feel safe, cared for. I experienced the same sense of safety at Girl Scout Camp, where we would often sing around a campfire at night, while making s'mores.

4

COURTSHIP

"Courtship is an old-fashioned word, assuming that two people who love each other will eventually get married."[15]

It seemed as if nothing in my life at home was ever easy. There were always two opposing forces operating, one healthy and the other decidedly not. On the one hand, Jamie's and my friendship was developing naturally into love; on the other, my father's behavior was often irrational, abusive, and out of control.

While there is more to say about my dad, it is easier to talk about Jamie and me. The summer when I was fourteen we spent time together but not to the exclusion of the others. Since Jamie was sixteen, his parents let him take their Chris Craft boat out, and he often gave me a ride in it. We would go to Lake George Village or up the lake, in order to steal a little time alone, but only occasionally. We were encouraged to spend time with the other kids.

On Labor Day that summer, Jamie and I were on his dock late in the afternoon. It was warm, and we were still in our bathing suits. Suddenly, without warning, Jamie kissed me on the cheek. Then he pushed me in the water. I was immensely pleased and surprised, but I wondered if he was embarrassed by the kiss, the very first.

I didn't want summer to end because he and I lived about 150 miles apart during the school year, but Jamie and I wrote to each other during this time. We talked about our classes, the World Series, and what songs were popular in our area. It was typical teenage talk, but our budding romance helped us get through high school. Having a boyfriend certainly took the pressure off me as far as dating, and the fact that Jamie lived near New York City only added to the mystique. I remember announcing to my tenth-grade biology teacher I knew who I was going to marry. She told me I would change my mind. "No, I won't," I told her. I knew I had found someone with whom I felt safe, someone who would not judge me for my family's problems or their effect on me.

Jamie even took the train to see me during the winter. I loved in-between visits like this. They felt like a gift. When it was time for him to leave, we often went to the railroad station where there was an embossing machine and made metal medallions with words on them. We wrote things like "Jamie and Susan forever." We still have some of them. Once, my father drove Jamie and me to the train station instead of my mom. I wanted to kiss Jamie goodbye, but as I approached him, he kept backing away with a big smile on his face. I could see it was a game. He thought it was funny, but on the way home, my father gave me a lecture about not chasing boys. I heard him, but I had stopped listening to him seriously, due to his earlier actions.

On my fifteenth birthday, my mother and I took a train to New York City to meet Jamie and his mom for lunch. We had tickets to see George Bernard Shaw's play, *Saint Joan*, on Broadway. Jamie and I held hands during the play, while my mother continually whispered, "Stop holding hands." Jamie's mom whispered back to her, "Be quiet; leave them alone." Jamie and I just smiled and ignored my mother. We felt such joy at seeing one another again. I remember how excited I was to see Jamie; I appreciated my mother making it possible.

Although my mom didn't like public displays of affection, she actually got a lot of pleasure out of Jamie's and my romance. She always liked him and did what she could to help us see one another. She sent mixed signals, though. There were times when Jamie and I were getting along fine and she would tell me, "There are many fish in the sea." But other times, when Jamie and I were at odds, she would say, "A bird in the hand is worth two in the bush." Despite this, she still made sure I could see Jamie.

A couple years later I went to Bronxville to Jamie's junior prom. He and I went out to dinner at a very nice place, but Jamie worried the whole time about whether he had enough money to pay the bill. I found his concern about money endearing, although I don't know why. I was not dressed like the other girls at the prom. I had on a long, net dress like we would wear to proms at home, but the girls at Jamie's school had on cocktail dresses, which were neither long nor made of net. Since Jamie didn't seem to care how different I looked, I figured I didn't need to care either. I think his acceptance gave me the confidence I needed.

The next year, at his senior prom, I decided to get smart and wear a party dress as the girls had done the previous year, but senior year they all wore the long, net dresses. I laughed as I made the same mistake twice. I was just happy to be with Jamie and counting down the days until summer when I could see him every day.

When Jamie and I were old enough to get summer jobs, we both worked, which was fine when my mom was there. But the weekend nights were difficult. With my mother gone, my brother and sister had jobs elsewhere, leaving my father and me alone. My mom would always tell me not to abandon my father. I felt like I was held responsible for his emotional well-being. I understand this situation is known as "parentification."[16]

Jamie came over with his guitar most nights and serenaded me. He was my protector. He and I always sat on the steps right outside the living room where my father was reading, which meant I wasn't leaving him alone. I used to love those evenings. Jamie left at bedtime, but I think the fact Jamie was next door protected me even after he left.

Throughout the year I just wanted to be with Jamie, who made me feel safe and cared for.

During Jamie's first year at the University of Rochester he invited me to his school's Fall Weekend event. I was amazed my parents let me go; I assume it was because I would be staying in the women's dorm. The idea of a college weekend with Jamie—with no parents around—thrilled me. I took the train to Rochester on Friday afternoon. The weekend flew by in a busy flurry. He was a pledge of a well-known national fraternity, and on Saturday we worked with some of the other pledges on a float for the football parade. In the afternoon we went to the game and then out to dinner before heading to the Fall Dance.

The Rochester girls had to be back in the dorm by 3 a.m. At the designated time I went to the front desk and said my boyfriend and I would like to sit downstairs and talk some more, but the lady in charge snapped, "Uh-uh. He goes home now." All I remember about the rest of the night was Jamie's friend Sue, with whom I was staying, served herself, her roommate, and me saké, a Japanese wine, which was god-awful. I couldn't drink it, but I got a kick out of being considered one of the big girls.

I couldn't wait until I could go to college after my weekend. When I decided on a school, it was Wells College on Cayuga Lake. It was as close to Rochester as my parents would allow me, but by his second year Jamie had a car and drove to Wells to see me almost every weekend.

A passage from one of my favorite books by renowned psychologist Dr. Bessel van der Kolk really speaks to me. He talks about the inner maps we all form when young about what is safe and what is dangerous. The maps are based on our experiences with our earliest caregivers. Van der Kolk says that our maps can be modified later in life. This can happen, for instance, because of a "deep love relationship, particularly during adolescence when the brain … goes through a period of exponential change [which] truly can transform us."[17]

I think my romance with Jamie was what allowed me to be happy during my high school years. When I was studying or talking to my friends, my father's continued abusive behavior seemed far away, and I suspect it was Jamie's love, which made the rest of it seem less important.

The joy was real. But there were still things I did during my high school years, which suggested something—the sexual abuse, for instance—may have been simmering just below the surface.

I became an ardent Episcopalian, for instance, and went to two Christian youth rallies where an official in front invited the congregation to come forward and be "saved." I went up to be saved twice because I didn't feel any healing after the first time. The truth is, though, I wasn't certain what to expect, but I am sure I felt "different" from the other kids there. The church was not equipped to handle an issue like abuse, I realize now, years later.

Because of my deepening feelings toward Jamie, I felt it necessary to tell him about the sexual abuse very early in our relationship. I was concerned he might see me as damaged and, therefore, unacceptable. I gave him the bare facts but no details. I wouldn't let him tell anybody or ask any questions either. This was a "test" to see whether he would be put off because of the abuse. I watched his face carefully when I told him, and he showed no evidence of rejection. I breathed a sigh of relief, as I was prepared to end our budding friendship if he reacted badly. But there was no problem.

5

OUT OF CONTROL

I am getting ahead of myself, for even Lake George was not spared my father's anger. No, I remember a time up there when my mom and dad had a rip-roaring fight. Their fights had largely ceased by then, making this one particular fight a surprise. They made enough noise in the middle of the night to wake my sister and me up. My father picked my mother up and was carrying her down to the lake to throw her in. She begged him to put her down. I don't think they had any idea how much noise they were making. Pretty soon the lights went on in Jamie's house next door, and Jamie's mild-mannered father yelled out the bedroom window, "For God's sake, put her down!" My parents were startled enough to think that anybody possibly heard them, causing my father to almost drop my mother.

The next day, two state policemen appeared on Jamie's dock. Unbeknownst to us, Jamie's parents found an abandoned boat in the bay and called the police about it. The officers were there in response to their call, but my mother thought they arrived because of her and my father's fight. She told Ann and me to hurry up from the dock and get in the car. We escaped before the officers could come over. Of course, this was never part of the policemen's plans.

The fight probably explains why my mom went home on weekends when my father arrived.

My dad was physically abusive to my sister as well. I remember watching him chase my sister outside our house at Lake George. Our cottage was situated on a small hill, and the ground was very rocky, which prevented him from moving quickly. Ann was more agile and was able to get away from him. At one point I confronted him, and he turned on me and said, "Would you like to have some of this too?" His look was evil, his eyes dark and empty.

I felt like I had to protect my sister, as she would have done the same for me. She was always more confrontational with my dad, ready to stand up to him. Sometimes I wished I had this quality too. My mom wasn't much help, as she was too frightened.

One time in Scotia, when Ann and I were in high school, I had been out and came home to see my mother standing in the kitchen by the stove. I could hear my sister's loud cries coming from the living room. I asked what was going on, but my mother didn't answer me. I went into the living room and saw my sister lying on her back on the rug. My father was sitting astride her stomach and hitting Ann about the face. In a rush of sympathy and anger, I took one look and yelled at my father, "You get off her!"

He looked at me in absolute amazement, like he was thinking, "Where did you come from? Why are you yelling?" He was startled enough he did get off her immediately. It was like I snapped him out of his fury for the moment.

My sister was sent away to school soon afterward. I always thought this was my mother's way of protecting her from our father. To my surprise, my mother asked me if I would like to go to private school too. I told her no, because it was my senior year, and I wanted to stay home with my friends. Little did I know what staying home would mean ... or I might have made a different choice.

This event may have marked the first time I really understood the extent of my mother's fear of my dad, who was big and physically aggressive. She had good reason to be afraid.

Everyone in the family was afraid of my father, I believe. Our neighbor once told us my dad was the angriest man he had ever encountered. I guess he physically abused everybody in our family but me. With me, the abuse was always sexual. Was I too docile and accommodating, too sweet and non-confrontational? Was I too easy a target?

During my last year at home, I was alone, of course. I showered and washed my hair every day around four in the afternoon. It was before hair dryers were commonly available for the home, and I wanted my hair to have plenty of time to dry before bed.

Once school started, my mother managed to be out most of the time, which meant she wouldn't be around until dinner time. This gave my father plenty of time to get home and satisfy his sexual urges by coming into my bathroom. He would move the shower curtain aside and watch me in the shower. I hated it … yet I seemed unable to do anything to counter it.

The simplest answer would have been for me to change the time of my shower to the evening when my mother was home. I wonder why I didn't consider this. Was I afraid my hair would not dry? Or my father would have bothered me in some other inappropriate manner while I was studying in the afternoon?

Equally easy would have been for me to tell my mother … or at least threaten to tell her. I could have done this too, although my intention was to leave my mother out of it to protect her and the rest of my family—and me too. I was afraid if I told her, she might have sent me away to school to stop the shower incidents.

I did neither of those things, but I found from researchers Carolyn Ainscough and Kay Toon a possible explanation for my inability to act. They noted that "the powerlessness experienced in sexual abuse can lead to long-term feelings of being unable to take action or change situations."[18]

Finkelhor and Browne would agree that "a basic kind of powerlessness occurs when a child's territory and body space are repeatedly [violated] against the child's will."[19]

How often, I wonder, did this sense of powerlessness render me unable to act? But I also learned not to ask for what I needed, and that plagued me for years afterward.

In fact, I never talked to anybody about the showers, although they went on daily for most of my senior year. They were a secret, just like the earlier abuse, only now I didn't even tell Jamie about them until years later.

As for my father, I had neither the courage nor the confidence to confront him myself. I only knew I did not trust him, and I felt deep inside that whatever he said or did in response would hurt me in ways I could only imagine. Being silent about the showers, though, made me feel like I *participated* in them. I felt guilty. I never tried to put a lock on the bathroom door because I thought he would remove it—or become physically violent.

I felt very depressed in the presence of my father. It felt like he was re-victimizing me every time he watched me. I remember I felt completely helpless and afraid of my father, as he was a powerful adult and the head of the family, and I was just a young person. My salvation was the fact I could escape very soon by heading off to college.

6

1958: DEAR GRANDMOMMY

I finally made it to college, where I could see Jamie every weekend, and I was away from the craziness at home, especially from my father. It sounded to me like a recipe for complete happiness. I was on my own and completely free. It was as wonderful as I hoped it would be!

Shortly after I arrived at Wells College, Jamie gave me his fraternity pin. Being pinned was considered a prequel to getting engaged. We were serious, and I was excited to show it off. But freshmen at Wells had to wear a cloth identification sign around their necks for the first six weeks of the school year, preventing anybody from seeing my pin. When the time was up, I went to my psychology class, a sophomore class I had requested special permission to attend. My professor said in front of everybody, "Aren't you a little young to be pinned?" I could have gone through the floor; I was terribly embarrassed. Still, I was committed to Jamie. I knew I wasn't too young.

On weekends Jamie and I managed to spend a lot of time alone, sometimes in his car, sometimes in a "date room" at my school. Jamie, with my agreement, decided it was time for us to engage in some sexual exploration. I trusted Jamie, but our activity always made me nervous. I didn't know what my problem was. I just knew I was uncomfortable until the activity ended. We started trying to talk through some of my issues, and I wrote him a few times about it.

In mid-November of my first year, Jamie called me in a panic. He had opened a letter from me, which began "Dear Grandmommy." I had switched the envelopes. My father's mother had received the letter I had intended for Jamie, a letter describing our sexual activities and my insecurities in detail. Jamie was mortified.

"Please don't worry about my grandmother," I said, as I tried to calm Jamie down. "The mistake has already been made, and there isn't any way to undo it." I had high hopes nothing would happen. Jamie was not convinced.

My confidence all would blow over was reinforced when my grandmother returned the original "Dear Jamie" letter she had received, noting *she had not read it*. I wrote Jamie immediately and remarked, "Isn't this fabulous?!"

But I was naïve to believe her. About two weeks later, I went home for Thanksgiving and drove with my father and sister to my grandmother's house in New Jersey. One night, I woke up and heard my father and grandmother come into my bedroom. I watched them take Jamie's fraternity pin from the top of the dresser. It made me angry, but I said nothing. The truth is I felt powerless with those two aligned against me. I believed they would ignore anything I said anyway.

Looking back, it was not only clear my grandmother *had lied* to me about the letter, but she had gotten my father upset as well. Still, neither of them said anything to me about the contents of the letter, their concerns, or asked me about anything. Their only idea was to remove Jamie from the picture!

Later a friend asked me if the letter mistakenly sent to my grandmother might have been a cry for help on my part because of the sexual issues. I assured her my grandmother and I were not at all close, and I never would have appealed to her under any circumstances.

On our way back home to the Schenectady area, my father made an unannounced detour, stopping at Jamie's home in Bronxville to return Jamie's fraternity pin. My father and Jamie's mother got into a shouting match on the sidewalk in front of their house. He accused Jamie of taking unwanted liberties with me.

I remember his mom telling my dad, "It takes two to tango!"

I was forbidden to see Jamie anymore. My father went far enough as to contact the Dean at Wells. He requested Jamie be banned from the campus, which the college was not set up to do—nor did they see it as their role.

Then he wrote Jamie a threatening letter. I still have the original. As you read this, remember this letter is written by the same man who abused me.

> "Of all the s.o.b.'s on Earth, the lowest louse is the seducer of young virgins. Young girls do not know how to handle their own emotions, therefore it is up to their men friendships to protect them, against themselves, if necessary. Fortunately there are laws in this State to protect young girls. You know, I am sure, you are laying yourself open to a possible life term in prison by associating with Susan; you yourself, being nineteen, are an adult. I have instructed the authorities at Wells you are not allowed to see Susan or communicate with her. If you try to, you will be arrested." (Emphases added.)

A couple of days later, my father sent a second long letter to Jamie apologizing for the initial one. I suspect the second one was a result of my mother's fury at the whole incident.

I was upset and depressed by these events. I had no idea how to undo the very real damage done by my father, or how to restore my relationship with Jamie, which was important to me.

A day or two after the blowup, I was still at home, and my mother asked me, out of the blue, "Would you like me to go to Rochester to see Jamie (who was back at school) to tell him everything will be all right?" I was amazed. "You would go there?" I asked. True to her word, within a few days, she drove there—about 140 miles—and basically told Jamie, who was disconsolate, not to worry because things would calm down.

▓▓▓▓▓▓▓▓▓

Schenectady, N Y
12-2-58

Dear Janie:

You and I have been friends a long time, and you deserve a letter
explaining the facts of life. When a girl marries she has babies,
and from then until they are grown up and leave home, she is
fully occupied raising and caring for them, and is in no position
to work outside. Why should you expect ▓▓▓▓ to do the
impossible? Why doesn't she deserve the same break in life that
your sisters each have, and that your Mother had? She is as good
as they are; she isn't some kind of servant. You have no right
to talk marriage to any girl until you are able to support her
and yourself. If you really loved her you would want to get a
job so you could marry her. That is what your Father did. But
you, on the other hand, have suddenly decided to extend your
schooling into the indefinite future. This eliminates you as
a candidate for marriage. When you and ▓▓▓▓▓ were children-
sweethearts I had no objection, but a free-love relationship
is out of the question. I was fascinated to hear your Mother
say that free love was all right. I suppose this accounts for
your lack of morality. Of all the s.o.b.'s on Earth, the
lowest louse is the seducer of young virgins. Young girls do
not know how to handle their own emotions, therefore it is up
to their men friends to protect them, against themselves if
necessary. Fortunately there are laws in this State to protect
young girls. You know, I am sure, that you are laying yourself
open to a possible life-term in prison by associating with
▓▓▓▓. You yourself, being 19, are an adult. I have
instructed the authorities at Wells that you are not to be
allowed to see ▓▓▓▓ or to communicate with her. If you
try to, you will be arrested. You cannot see her here, nor
will she come to Bronxville nor to Rochester. If you should
in some way become self-supporting, you can let me know of the
change, if you should then wish to become a suitor for ▓▓▓▓s
hand in marriage.

Very truly yours,

▓▓▓▓▓▓▓▓

My mom was a lifesaver! She always liked Jamie, which may have helped. My mom seemed to have parented me much more than she did my brother and sister. I mean like her driving all the way to Jamie's school to console him. Maybe it was because of Jamie, who was a favorite, or maybe it had something to do with the fact I was docile. My sister was more of a fighter.

My mom and I certainly had our issues over the years, but she and I ended up friends, much more than she did with my brother and sister. Once I realized she was afraid of my father, I was able to understand her behavior better. And I eventually forgave her for the ways she failed me.

I was always grateful for our friendship. After my mom's trip to Rochester, things did calm down. Still, I was always wary of my father. His behavior was completely irrational at times. I think he must have been very jealous of Jamie.

7

INDEPENDENCE:
A MIXED BLESSING

On my second day at Wells College, I stepped on a scale and saw I had lost half a pound. I said to myself, "I think I'll go on a diet." At the time, I had no idea where my thought came from; it was completely new to me. Nevertheless, those words, voiced carelessly in my head, ended up dictating my dietary habits for most of my life. Henceforth, I consciously avoided eating fats and, for a time, most carbohydrates. In college I allowed myself to eat meat, vegetables, fruit, eggs, cottage cheese, and dry cereal, as much as I wanted; but I was not taking in enough calories. I lost 25 pounds, going from 114 down to 89, which resulted in the cessation of my periods. I was hungry all the time, but I believed I was just experiencing indigestion, not hunger.

Van der Kolk characterized this experience well when he said "trauma results in a fundamental reorganization of ... the mind ... It changes not only how we think and what we think about, but also our capacity to think."[20]

If anyone had asked me why I curtailed my diet so drastically, I didn't have an answer. No, I was a healthy weight at the time, and the need for a diet was never mentioned at home or with my friends. Even now, looking back at it, it made no sense for me to go on a crash diet. It seems to me like a perfect example of my inability to think about what I was doing or, especially, *why I was doing it*. Yet I stubbornly adhered to my idea. I was very rigid about what I would or would not eat.

My unnecessary, unplanned weight loss attracted attention. Jamie, for instance, frequently made me promise to gain weight. I may have pacified him by agreeing, but I never gained any weight. The worst was when I went home. My parents reacted badly. My father's solution was to, once again, write the dean of my school and request I be weighed every week. The dean and I complied. The nurse weighed me faithfully on schedule, but nobody talked to me about my diet or asked me, "Why aren't you eating?" I don't know what she would have done if she had asked the question and I had no answer. My family was looking for someone to blame. My father blamed Jamie, as did my sister; but I knew it had nothing to do with Jamie.

I was seeing doctors at the time, but they neither asked me questions nor gave me a diagnosis. In fact, nobody was talking about eating disorders at the time.

When I went home the first summer, my parents made me eat, which happened simply because I was not up to arguing with them about it. I remembered clearly how violent my father could be, and I wanted none of his wrath. I, therefore, gained several pounds with them and proceeded to lose it all when I went back to school for my second year.

8

RESEARCH NOTES ON ANOREXIA AND CHILD SEXUAL ABUSE

I learned much later of a substantial amount of research available, which confirms a distinct causal link between child sexual abuse and eating disorders like anorexia. It was a surprise to me as I had never made the connection.

Numerous studies about this association have been published, but before we continue, I need to make sure the meaning of anorexia is clear.

Anorexia nervosa is defined by the Social Work Dictionary as a potentially life-threatening disorder found primarily "in girls and young women in whom the extended refusal to eat leads to severe weight loss, malnutrition, and cessation of menstruation."[21] The usual medical criteria include the loss of one-fourth or more of one's body weight.

In fact, I reminded Jamie doctors evaluated me in the late fifties concerning my weight, and nobody ever mentioned anorexia to me.

Most of the research linking sexual abuse and eating disorders seemed to begin with eating-disordered clients, who were then queried about earlier sexual abuse. For instance, a study by Mary Anne Cohen, head of an eating disorder clinic in New York, discovered some 40–60% of the people in her clinic had been sexually or physically abused.[22]

Similarly, others found some 50% of the anorexic and bulimic patients they interviewed had a history of child sexual abuse compared to 29% in a control population.[23]

There are still other studies, which find an affirmative link between the two; they are too many to mention but one of these groups reported: "… the data do suggest individuals who display impulsive behavior following the abuse may be more likely to show disordered eating."[24]

In Cohen's 1995 insightful book, *French Toast for Breakfast*, she observed that the sexual abuse and eating disorder link is forged by the survivor's feelings of "… guilt, shame, anesthesia, self-punishment, soothing, comfort, protection, and rage."[25] She uses the term "emotional eating," which she says means, "being hungry from the heart, not the stomach."[26] Cohen continues with the idea eating problems are used to "communicate matters of the heart, which have no other channel [of expression]."[27] She notes that emotional eating refers to the use of "food to distract, detour, or deny inner problems; to anesthetize oneself to protect from pain. It is safer to achieve intimacy … with food than with a partner."[28]

She continues, noting the anorexic who is "incapable of discharging her hostility directly … unconsciously initiates a process of slow suicide. Her starvation becomes an aggressive act to punish the parent …"[29]

Another study notes that "survivors may … react to feeling powerless by attempting to take control and by making themselves feel more powerful in some way. Eating disorders then involve a desperate attempt to exert some control by controlling one's food intake and body weight."[30]

I told Jamie I was fascinated by these statements. *I have realized, years later, mine was not an idle act. It was a way to get back at my father! I must have been very angry with him, causing me to starve myself to punish him for leering at me in the shower.*

Later Cohen describes some of the reasons survivors follow this route; for instance, they often turn to dieting to relieve the stress and tension of the trauma. Some of these very thin survivors starve and purge in order to create "perfect" bodies, which make them feel "more powerful, invulnerable, and in control," making up for the helpless feeling in childhood.[31]

Much earlier, Hilde Bruch in her book, *The Golden Cage*, believed young women are trying to undo the "bodily aspects of adolescent changes through excessive thinness" in order to interrupt a "development in which they [feel] troubled."[32]

Again this makes great sense to me, I told Jamie, as I suspect this is why my father was gaping at me in the shower!

To continue, Bruch notes that the psychological functioning of the anorexic is disturbed in three particular areas: (1) she suffers from a "severe disturbance in body image;" (2) she experiences a "misinterpretation of internal … stimuli," including an "inaccuracy in the way hunger is experienced;" (3) she feels "a sense of ineffectiveness, the conviction of being helpless to change anything about her life."[33]

The quote reminds me of my experience. First, I misunderstood my hunger and, since I thought it was indigestion, it never occurred to me to do anything to correct this problem. And, second, I seemed unable to change the shower scene during my last year at home. It was almost as if I was resigned to them.

According to Bruch, many anorexics blame their bodies for their discomfort and blame themselves for their shortcomings. They punish themselves by denying themselves food. The loss of weight doesn't concern them because they have a "distorted body image." They do not "see" how emaciated they are.[34]

I remember telling Jamie when I looked at myself in the mirror, I was unable to see how thin I was. I thought I looked fine.

I can now understand why I stopped eating and lost weight. Angry at my father's abuse, I developed a case of full-blown anorexia, long before the disorder was defined or recognized in our country. The doctors I saw were completely puzzled by my symptoms and could neither give me a diagnosis nor suggest a treatment.

It was in college where my eating disorder was most virulent. But I was to discover during my life that my anorectic symptoms abated at times, while at other times the disorder went through stages or phases. When I first married and had young children, for instance, I ate normal meals with Jamie and the children. This period lasted almost twenty years until I began teaching Jeffrey and Rachel at home and decided I needed some free time to myself, with no one else around, to unwind from the day's activities. I thus developed a new stage in eating, which was bizarre. I ate only one meal a day, late at night. All I ate was a carton of pineapple ice milk, which I consumed while lying on the floor reading. Often tired enough, I would fall asleep while eating.

I believe this stage was simply a modification of the earlier anorexia. I adapted my eating behavior to meet my current needs.

The stage lasted for several years until the one-year anniversary of Jeffrey's death. I used the occasion to change my eating behavior again and begin a new stage. I made a decision to re-unite and participate with my family's mealtimes by eating three meals daily with them, no longer alone. Why I made this choice remains a mystery, but I continued to avoid fats at all costs. It was the way I was able to keep my weight low, which was, for me, my main concern.

At this point, I believed I met a goal by once again joining my family in eating. I thought I completed the work I had to do and was now eating freely, like other people. Only my family was aware I was skimping on fats.

I found my behavior satisfactory enough I could have done it forever, but eventually, in 2019, fate intervened. Jamie had a serious bicycle accident which almost killed him. He was hospitalized at Duke Hospital for five weeks, followed by five weeks of rehabilitation, after which he thankfully survived. For those weeks I lived at my daughter's home, which was close to where Jamie was being treated. I would remain at Jamie's side during the day and return in the evening for dinner. Since Rachel did all the cooking, I ate what was served. I had to abandon my no-fats preference as I was a guest and in no position to make special requests. This situation allowed me to savor the full flavor of many foods, and I found I actually enjoyed the experience. I believe this was the final step in my letting go of my life-long anorexic habits. I realized once again that eating is, in addition to ingesting calories, a social activity, and there are many, many really delicious foods! Now, after all these years, I enjoy eating again.

9

EMBRACING RISK

*Van der Kolk notes that "… abuse in adolescence
was significantly associated only with anorexia nervosa
and with increased risk-taking."*[35]

*Author Sue Blume found that "many incest survivors …
may be inclined toward high-risk behavior, daring the fates."*[36]

As I have discussed my issues with anorexia, I have learned it is considered very risky behavior because of the resulting relatively high rates of mortality. When I curtailed my diet, though, I certainly did not understand the danger.

There were other times when I was also unaware of situations that were risky. Shortly after we were married, Jamie was taking a bath and asked me to bring the radio into the bathroom as he wanted to listen to it. I brought in both the radio and an extension cord, letting the end of the live wire drop into the bath water. Jamie shot out of the tub as it occurred. Thankfully, nothing happened to him, but he had to explain to me the danger of mixing electric current and water. I was horrified, but nobody ever taught me about the danger, which means it doesn't count as intentional risky behavior.

Other times I knew the risk and chose to ignore it. Smoking is a good example. I began smoking just occasionally in college, but I became increasingly addicted as time went on. It is another example, though, where I am actually not certain the risky action was associated with anything in my past. A great many people used to smoke.

I began smoking more after I started having children. One of my daughters convinced me to give it up. I have not had a cigarette now in decades.

As I got older, I became more comfortable with risk. For example, I used to deliberately leave my keys in the car, figuring I wouldn't lose them that way when I went to the store. I didn't worry about it until the day when I finished shopping and went back to look for the car, and it was gone. Luckily it had just been stolen by a couple of boys, who took it for a joy ride and left it in an empty field undamaged.

Another example of a considered risk I took was at Lake George. One morning before work, I decided to go for a swim. It was only seven o'clock; my mother wasn't up yet, and nobody else was moving around. I planned to swim by myself across the head of Dunham's Bay, about half a mile round trip. I realized this idea had a certain amount of risk, but it was a calculated risk. I was a strong swimmer. Since my father and I would swim a total of a mile every weekend, I wasn't concerned about the distance. The one problem I could face was meeting boats traveling down the bay to the boathouse, but the early hour made it unlikely. I did the swim, and it was fine. In fact, I was really pleased with myself once it was done.

But I have yet to tell you my favorite story. It was another calculated risk. I had a boss who drove a motorcycle; he gave me a ride, and I was immediately hooked. I asked, and Jamie very sweetly agreed, to get himself a motorcycle. He became a very good, very safe driver, and he was happy to give me rides. We lived near the Blue Ridge Parkway at the time and had a perfect place to ride. Since the speed limit there is only 45 mph and there is little traffic, we were about as safe as one can be on a motorcycle. As I rode on the back of Jamie's bike, I discovered I enjoyed the curvy roads to and from the Parkway as much or more than the Parkway itself.

Before long I decided I wanted to drive my own motorcycle. We bought a small bike, and I began learning to drive, with Jamie as my teacher. I was fearful at first and would only drive up the very small hill in the backyard. I relaxed as I realized I could control the bike. None of it came easily to me, but I kept at it until I became more confident. I still remember the day I took the test for my motorcycle license. I was a nervous wreck and stopped way too short of the stopping line, but the tester turned a blind eye and passed me anyway.

I was now ready to accompany Jamie on trips to the Blue Ridge Parkway, which we did frequently. It made a nice daytrip. I soon discovered, as we traveled the winding roads to the Parkway, I could increase my pleasure with a certain maneuver. I would slow down before we reached a curve, then speed up. I would be going fast enough I could lean the bike over very far, far enough to scrape the foot pegs on the pavement. Jamie rode ahead of me, and he told me later he had heard this noise the first time I did it and couldn't figure out what it was. I got such a thrill out of leaning the bike way over. I became addicted to the behavior until someone informed me that if my foot peg encountered a stick or some other object on the pavement, I could be thrown from the bike and even killed. It didn't take me long afterward to realize continuing this behavior was too big a risk. But here, once knowing the risks, I modified my behavior, but it was tough stopping. Unlike other risks I took in the past, riding my bike required me to work hard to master a skill. I was very proud of my riding ability because of the effort. When I got a bigger bike and had trouble making slow turns, I still loved it. I think the bike represented pure enjoyment to me, plus a sense of freedom and the chance to experience nature and the open road. I definitely enjoyed the identity of being a motorcycle driver. I loved every single time I parked the bike, took off my helmet, and heard somebody exclaim in amazement that I was not only female, but also a small, older one. The best response was the surprise of young girls. I always figured I could be a role model for them of some type of gender equality.

Jamie and I used to have discussions about the difference in people's comfort level with risk. I have always been more comfortable with it than Jamie has, and I still am.

10

1960: LIVING THE DREAM

In college, I saw Jamie most weekends; but I remember even then I wanted to see him more often. What I needed was the daily contact, which comes from sharing a life and sharing a home.

I am not exactly certain why we made the decision to marry when we did. Jamie never proposed; it was just understood we would be together. We often talked about 1960 as the year we would do it, after I finished two years of college and Jamie finished three. A few years before our wedding, we even made a medallion on an embossing machine at the Schenectady railroad station printed with our names plus the date, May 29, 1960. We didn't have a plan to get married then; we just picked a date and made the medallion for fun.

We went through a formal engagement during spring break of my sophomore year, and Jamie's parents came up to be with us. I still remember his mom coming through our front door, saying as she greeted me, "I hope you like the ring." It was an old family ring, but the diamonds had been reset in a Tiffany setting. There is a central diamond with diamond chips circling the center giving it the appearance of a flower. I loved it instantly.

When I returned to Wells, people were very interested in the ring and in our wedding plans. The Dean even called me in for a chat. She happened to have been in Schenectady over the break and had seen the engagement announcement in the paper. She sat me down and asked,

"However did you get your parents to allow your engagement?" I thought about my father's letter to her a year earlier about keeping Jamie and me apart, and I wanted to laugh. I was at a loss as to what to say. It would have taken me a week to explain my parents to her, even had I felt up to the task. I elected instead to answer nonchalantly, "Oh, they were very happy," which did not make her any wiser but may have reminded her of the extremely strange ways of some people.

My Wells friends gave me a shower before I left in May, and I bought my wedding dress. It was a lovely gown of embroidered nylon over taffeta, with a fitted bodice and a bouffant skirt with several tiers in the back. I thought it was beautiful and felt beautiful in it!

The next couple of months were a whirlwind of activity, notifying bridesmaids and purchasing their dresses, which were made of pale yellow or pale green organza with a deeper-colored sash. There were several more showers, one given by Jamie's sisters, and another one I remember particularly because of the rum punch. The drink was made by pouring rum over lime sherbet, which was delicious. My sister Ann certainly enjoyed it. I don't know how many glasses she drank, but she was feeling exceptionally good by the end of the party.

Our wedding was in mid-July. It was a beautiful day. I was very nervous in the back of the church before I walked down the aisle. My brother was an usher, and I squeezed his hand tightly. I heard later that my grandmother in the front row was muttering "rats, rats, rats" during the service. It was a good thing I didn't hear her, or I would have gone down to her seat and suggested she leave if she was unhappy. But now I'm not actually sure what she meant.

Ann told me recently what had upset my grandmother was the word "obey" in the wedding service when the woman promises "to love, honor, and obey" her husband. Since I was focused on getting married, I paid scant attention to the wording. But I know there are plenty of young women today, my daughters included, who are adamant about removing the word "obey" from the service.

We had a short reception, at which I was busy greeting people—and excited enough—I didn't have much time to eat. Jamie's best man, who was at least 6'7", and I, in my wedding dress, ended up doing the Charleston. It seemed just a few minutes before it was time to head upstairs and dress.

Jamie and I headed to Hyannis, Massachusetts, with plans to take the ferry boat to Nantucket Island in the morning. Prior to our wedding, the ferry boat company had been hit by a strike from its workers. Since most vacationers had simply canceled their reservations, Jamie and I ended up being the only people staying at our hotel on Nantucket. Our room had two single beds, and we tied them together as best we could. We spent an idyllic week there on the beaches, with no responsibility except to enjoy ourselves. I, at last, felt completely free to enjoy sex with Jamie. Without realizing it at the time, my problem all along had been due to issues with my father. Once I had the marriage certificate in hand, the fear of my dad and the anxiety were gone.

At the end of the week we headed back to Jamie's parents' place at Lake George for the rest of the summer. There was a small bunkhouse next to the main house where Jamie had always stayed, and he and I returned there. Jamie got his job back working as an orderly at the local hospital, and I was free to amuse myself. His mom and one of his sisters were there, too, and I enjoyed their company. I had known them long enough they were like family, at least family away from my dad.

Married life suited me. I had the love and support of someone who was unquestionably on my side. Jamie and I loved to spend time together, enjoying each other's company. We were in love, and I felt completely safe!

In the fall, we left Lake George and headed to Rochester as Jamie needed to finish his last year of college. I stopped going to school full-time and found a day job at the library on the University of Rochester campus. From there I followed Jamie to graduate school in Maryland and tried a couple of jobs, which were non-starters before I ended up working at the American Geophysical Union in Washington, D.C. I worked in the publications office, mainly doing proofreading.

Being married was wonderful.

11

VULNERABLE AGAIN

As psychiatrist Judith Herman said:
"The most important factor universally cited by [rape]
survivors is good luck."[37]

Although my sister Ann and I are close in age, we were in competition for years. When I was in sixth grade, Ann grew taller than I, and I think it may have been the beginning of the competition for her. She wanted to have her period first and be the first to get married, but I beat her on both measures. Ann did have the first baby, though, a good two years before Jamie and I had our first child.

After Ann's son was born, my mother and I decided to take the train to Chicago to see her and the new baby. My mother stayed in a motel, but I slept at Ann's place. Since Ann's husband was a student at the University of Chicago, they lived near the campus. I quickly learned it was not a safe neighborhood.

On a bright, sunny Sunday morning I decided to walk to church before meeting up with my mom. It was about 9:45 a.m. when I started out. I walked down the sidewalk, and I remember passing by a man working under the hood of his car. Suddenly, without warning, a large hand came from somewhere behind me and covered my mouth. It was unexpected and took my brain a few seconds to register the attack; then I was terrified! I had not heard anybody come up behind me!

The hand belonged to a very large, black man. He literally dragged me backwards down the sidewalk, my heels scraping the pavement as he pulled me along. *Where was the person working on his car*, I wondered, as panic took over. Where was anybody who could help? I could not see a soul on the street. The attacker dragged me into an empty, unfurnished, street-level apartment nearby. Then he locked the door and took his hand from my mouth.

I stayed very calm outwardly, but my brain was reeling. The only coherent thought running through my head was that I would never see Jamie again. I believed this man was going to kill me. I didn't know what his motive was. I assumed it was robbery, but the violence of the attack gave me a very bad feeling in the pit of my stomach. I had always told myself I would yell if someone attacked me, but it was clear to me at the moment yelling for help was a very bad idea. There didn't seem to be anybody around to hear me shouting, and I did not want to make this man angry.

I didn't have my purse with me or any money, which may have thrown him. The only thing I had was my half of the Mizpah coin my husband and I wore around our necks. It is a "coin" split unevenly into two pieces which fit together and say, "May the Lord watch between me and thee when we are apart, one from the other." The man asked me about it, but he didn't take it. I told him, without mentioning my husband. I was twenty-one, but when he asked me my age, I told him I was fourteen years old. I was small enough, and I looked young. Luckily, he never saw my wedding ring.

As he faced me, he pulled off my stockings, panties, and garter belt and inserted his finger in my vagina. I didn't know if he intended right then to rape me. If he did, he changed his mind.

The apartment we were in was bare. We were standing on a hard cement floor without even a carpet. Maybe it was our surroundings, or maybe it was my alleged age, but all I know is he said, "Wait a minute," went to the door, unlocked it, and then disappeared through it. I didn't trust he was truly gone. I waited for what seemed like forever before I opened the door and looked around. I saw nobody, and I went back to my sister's apartment.

It was decidedly jarring—to be under attack and then freed quickly with no explanation. I was upset also that I could not bring this man to justice, but I was very relieved to have gotten away with my life.

I have no idea why he left, why he didn't complete whatever plan he had made, or why he didn't kill me. It is tempting to say God was watching out for me, but what would my relief say about the hundreds of women who were not as fortunate as I was? I thought about the women who ended up raped or brutally beaten or killed.

I felt fortunate because I survived when I thought I would not. I didn't report the crime. I was afraid the man would come back and seek revenge on my sister's family, as unrealistic as this sounds. Plus, the only identifying features I could remember were that the man was big and black, nothing else. I have thought about the event many times. Why didn't I notice more? I believe the explanation lay in the terror I felt. I didn't even maintain eye contact with him. Since I was focused on trying to figure out what he wanted and how to keep him from hurting me, I didn't pay attention to the details of his face. I was concentrating too hard on my own thoughts about how to stay safe. I stayed calm, for instance, in the face of terror, which allowed me to think about what I needed to do.

I was fortunate also not to have nightmares or panic attacks afterwards. I was only left with a sense of hyper vigilance. But I have always turned around since and looked when I heard someone walking behind me. The terror of the sudden, unseen hand over the mouth, coming from behind, has stayed with me all these years!

Afterwards, I told my sister what happened, and her husband went with me while I showed him the apartment where I had been dragged. My undergarments were still there, as if to corroborate my story. I then called Jamie, just to hear his voice, the voice I thought I would never hear again. I didn't tell him about the attack on the phone. There was nothing he could do long distance, and I was afraid of how he would react.

The next day my mother and I went home. Not long afterwards a man with a gun came into Ann's apartment and told her to take off all of her clothes. Ann very coolly went out on the balcony and yelled for help. Hearing that, the man fortunately left. Ann and her family moved out of the area soon afterward. It wasn't worth the risk.

For both of us, I am very thankful the situations ended without either of us actually getting raped ... or killed!

The man who victimized me was the second person to do so, the first being my father. I can't help but compare the two events.

In both cases, I was blindsided by the confrontation. But the differences between the Chicago attack and the abuse by my father are vast: they include the mode of attack, my immediate reaction, and the long-term effect each had on me.

In Chicago, the man used his physical strength to overpower me in an initially violent assault. He wanted to isolate me. My father, on the other hand, didn't need to use physical force. His weapon was his relationship with me. I suspect it was the difference in the male's initial approach that caused the variations in my immediate response.

My father's action was a betrayal of trust, which left me stunned and unable to think or even feel. The man in Chicago threatened me, but I was able to stay calm and—within the limits of the situation—figure out the "safest" response to the attack and the attacker.

With my dad, I was much younger and I had no way to respond, nowhere to turn for help. All I could do was try to bury the incident in my memory.

There is another factor at play here. In Chicago I was able to return to a safe home soon after the attack, which is important. Dr. van der Kolk talks about "people [who] are terribly overwhelmed [and] start running ... and the direction is for home. If you can run home and ... people say ... "Let me take care of you," then you will be in much better shape."[38]

It is almost exactly what I did in response to the attack in Chicago. But there was no place for me to return and be safe when I was abused as a child.

12

AND BABY
MAKES THREE

I had been working almost three years in Washington D.C. when I discovered I was pregnant. I remember I was overjoyed at the thought of adding a baby to the mix. My due date was January 6, which is Epiphany, or Twelfth Night, according to the church calendar. I always kidded my daughter, telling her I was going to name her Epiphany and call her Piph! But I didn't actually go into labor until mid-January. We timed the contractions at home until 11 p.m. and then headed to the hospital as Jamie announced, "Our lives will never be the same."

I knew nothing about babies or labor, and the hospital environment was hardly supportive. When we arrived, I had to spend five hours alone in a hospital room. I had nobody to talk to, nobody who could encourage me by telling me I was doing a good job.

My doctor was at home sick at the time with a temperature of 103 degrees, which was unfortunate. The hospital policy was that my husband, who was sitting patiently in the waiting room, was not allowed to visit me until the doctor appeared. The nurses were mostly absent. The only time one of them came in, she asked how close my contractions were. When I told her I didn't know because I couldn't see the wall clock, she responded, "You have to do better than that. Put your glasses on; that way you can see the clock and time the contractions." Then she left.

I was unaware of the stages of labor then, but I recognized when the contractions were stronger and coming closer together. I learned much later this is the transition phase, which is the hardest part of labor. I started thinking I may not be able to bear much more pain when the intensity of the labor suddenly eased up. Something inside me said I would feel better if I started pushing, which I did. I pushed for some time before a nurse came in. She took one look, saw the baby's head was crowning and yelled, "Stop pushing!" I was rushed into the delivery room when my doctor miraculously appeared. He rattled off instructions to the nurses in the room and told me I needed a spinal anesthetic. I had already gone through 95% of the labor and told him I didn't want an anesthetic, but he didn't listen, and I was too tired to argue with him.

My spinal was much too late in the process. I could not feel the birth at all or help with the pushing. When they wheeled me back into my room, I was freezing cold, but I couldn't even move enough to reach the call button to ask for more blankets.

When they wheeled Maria in and I could see the baby, she was beautiful and sleeping soundly, probably from the drug.

I had other problems with the hospital. I asked the nurses if I could watch them bathe the baby, a lesson for me in how to do it. I thought it was a simple request and part of the hospital's mission to help new mothers learn how to care for their infants. I was wrong! The nurses flatly refused to teach me about baby baths. I can't remember if they tried to help me with nursing the baby, but as I dressed to go home, one nurse told me, "You can't nurse the baby. You'll have her right back here with jaundice." She thought, because I was a new mother, I would not produce enough milk, which was her way of telling me. I went home in tears. "I don't know what to do with my baby," I thought. "I don't know how to take care of her."

Fortunately, parenting a new baby is not difficult. For the first three months, Maria ate, slept, and produced messy diapers. She developed colic and cried from 2 a.m. until about 4 a.m. I tried everything to calm her down and finally, too weary to continue, I would fall asleep next to her.

I felt overwhelmed by the realization I was responsible for a new life—a new responsibility and a heavy one!

As I focused on Maria, I began skimping on self-care. As psychologist Christine Courtois notes, "Depression may result in a disregard for personal hygiene and a drab and unkempt personal appearance."[39] It got bad enough Jamie wanted to find professional help for me and my depression. He asked my parents for money to send me to psychotherapy, but they refused, which meant nothing changed. It is known that, when major stresses occur such as the birth of a child, past memories of abuse can occur.[40]

I introduce my first child, Maria, to her [maternal] grandfather.

I found caring for a new baby led to some scary moments for me. I was vacuuming under Maria's crib once when she was sleeping, and I was surprised the sound of the vacuum didn't awaken her. I was genuinely worried about whether Maria might be deaf. When she woke up, I blew up a balloon and popped it next to her ear. Poor Maria. It startled her mercilessly, and she burst into tears. I felt terribly guilty afterward.

There was another time when Maria was a little older she and I went out shopping. In the middle of our trip, I had to stop back home for a minute. I left Maria in the car while I hurried into the house. When I came back out, there was no car in the driveway. I went running out, and there was Maria, standing up in the front seat of the car, across the street from our house. I hadn't put the emergency brake on, and Maria had moved the shift lever from park to neutral. The driveway was on enough of a slant the car rolled slowly backwards. Maria looked surprised, but fortunately, unhurt. Thankfully, no car had come down the street while ours was in the road. I made an honest, if dumb, mistake, but the same thing happened all over again on another occasion. I didn't learn my lesson the first time!

This takes me back to my discussion of risk-taking. Did I, for some reason, not recognize the risk, even after Maria rolled down the driveway and into the street the first time? Apparently not. I wondered about it and where my mind was. It was appalling to think I could repeat the same error all over again. Was I disconnected enough from my actions to fail to observe the consequences of them? It was kind of scary when I started questioning what I was thinking. On my own, I tried to get my head back on straight.

About then, I enrolled in night school at the University of Maryland and took a course every semester in pursuit of my Bachelor's degree. I also found a part-time job as an admitting clerk Friday and Saturday nights at the hospital where Maria was born. The night I was trained, a nurse showed me a 3 x 5 card on the desk and said, "Since this pregnant young lady has not paid her pre-hospital bill, do not admit her if she comes in, even if she is in labor." I heard her with a great deal of trepidation. When she left, I turned to another nurse standing nearby and asked, "What do I do if this girl shows up?" "You admit her, of course," the second nurse answered. I breathed a sigh of relief.

My plan to work was good for my mood, but it involved working two night shifts per week. I was not making up the sleep I lost. One Monday, I put Maria down for her afternoon nap and then lay down myself. The next thing I knew it was 6 p.m., and Jamie was home from school.

"Where is Maria?" he asked me. Poor Maria was safely asleep in her crib, but I wondered how many times she had called to me after her nap. I felt terrible and realized I could not handle an overnight job without making up the sleep.

I took a break from working nights and started looking for a day job instead. I knew I wouldn't be able to make much money, and I didn't want to spend what I did earn on babysitting, but I needed to get out of the house to keep my spirits up. I wrote an advertisement for reciprocal babysitting and submitted it to the University of Maryland student newspaper. I received only one answer to the ad. It was from a young woman named Vicki, who had a baby a few months older than Maria.

She and I became good friends. She was in graduate school for social work. I babysat for her when she went to class, and she did the same for me when I had to work.

Much later I learned Vicki was not always in school when I babysat; sometimes she was involved in an extramarital liaison. Vicki and her husband Jack were a couple from the 1960s. They were in an open marriage.

Despite the differences in our sexual mores, I liked Vicki. She was a nice, kind, intelligent person, and she was good to Maria. Jamie and I began seeing Vickie and Jack on weekends, going to the zoo, riding bikes, cooking out, and just enjoying one another. I felt myself coming back to the present and my mood lifting.

PART

2 CHALLENGING TIMES

*My son's allergies cause him to cough ferociously
night and day … anxious and depressed, I seek comfort in
the arms of a friend … my marriage threatened …
sometime later I take the kids and run away …*

13

THE DREAM CONTINUES

In April 1968, when Maria was three and a half years old, Jamie finished his doctorate at the University of Maryland and decided to do a one-year post-doctorate at Johns Hopkins in Baltimore. We left our little house in College Park and moved to an apartment east of Baltimore in a very small town called Middle River. We were living there when Martin Luther King was shot. Some of the people in our area were in a celebratory mood the night of his killing. It was very upsetting.

Jamie's previous adviser from Maryland invited us to a party in College Park, and we drove down the Baltimore-Washington Parkway toward D.C. There was ongoing rioting in Washington after King's death, and part of the city was in flames. We followed military trucks traveling south on the Parkway from Fort Meade. We could see soldiers inside with their rifles at the ready. It was a sobering sight.

A few days after the riots in Washington, the unrest spread to Baltimore. A curfew was imposed in the county starting at 4 p.m. Each afternoon we went out on our balcony to look around. There were no cars in sight and no people. It was a very troubled time.

I became even more on edge when I found out I was pregnant! I had suffered two miscarriages after my first child, and I was petrified until I made it through the first three critical months. Once I did, everything seemed fine, and I started making plans. I wanted to have a home delivery because I had been unhappy in the hospital during

Maria's birth. It took some time, but I finally found a female doctor who agreed to a home delivery. My heart broke when she told me she was going to be out of the country on my due date, but she was a marvel. She exclaimed, "It's all right. I'll just induce labor!" It was as simple as she made it sound.

On the appointed day, Jamie took Maria out for the afternoon, and the doctor arrived at our place and proceeded to set up the Pitocin drip to induce labor. The contractions began, and she checked me periodically until it was time for the delivery. She delivered our son by herself and weighed him on a hand-held scale, not unlike those used to weigh vegetables in a market. After cleaning the baby and me, the doctor had to drive back to her office to pick up sutures, which her nurse had forgotten to put in her bag. She left Jeffrey and me alone in a sleepy stupor and then returned to finish up.

This was much better than the hospital, and our second child was a boy! I was delighted. I knew a lot about little girls, both from having Maria and from my own childhood, but I knew nothing about little boys. Jeffrey, as he grew, would be the one to introduce me to his world.

Maria was at a cute age; we were developing a family, and I felt satisfied. It was at this time that we moved from our apartment to a house in Silver Spring, Maryland, near where Jamie would be working.

My satisfaction was short-lived, though. Jeffrey was fine for six months; then he started having respiratory allergies. The allergies gave him chronic bronchitis during the winter. He would cough and cough. It sounded as if he was going to cough his insides out. Hearing it was excruciating. We took him to doctors, and they prescribed a medicine, which Jeffrey hated; and it didn't seem to help much anyway. I was a nervous wreck every night, listening to him cough. Nothing seemed to help. He felt bad. He had no energy at all.

I felt helpless. We were simply unable to stop Jeffrey's heart-wrenching coughs, a sound that made me extremely anxious and depressed. I remember being mildly depressed at Maria's birth, but my present despondency was far worse.

As I was depressed, I used the walls in our vestibule to copy some pretty disheartening quotes, like William Faulkner's, "But who loved death above all, who loved only death." I think I was afraid Jeffrey would die.

For four winters he was lethargic and dragged himself around, feeling bad; and we suffered with him. It was awful.

But Jeffrey recovered eventually, and we had our good times together. I remember once when he was young and just beginning to express himself, I took him shopping at the market. I wheeled him from aisle to aisle, and when we reached the laundry soap, Jeffrey took one look at the huge boxes of soap and told me: "I know what the big box of Tide is for — FAT people!"

Ah, I thought, *my son is figuring out how the world works.*

He had a wonderful sense of humor, just like his dad's. One night, when he was two, we were putting him to bed. Jamie, to be funny, jumped into Jeffrey's crib before he did and lay down, clutching his blanket. Jeffrey suddenly fell down on the bedroom rug, holding his stomach and groaning. Jamie jumped out of the crib, saying, "Jeffrey, what's wrong?" And before you could blink an eye, Jeffrey bounded up and was in his crib. We stood there with our mouths open. He had tricked us!

As he got older, he was interested in everything. Jeffrey liked all kinds of transportation vehicles and construction equipment. He liked dinosaurs, electricity, machines, and discovering how the world worked in general. He especially liked football because Jamie did. He learned the names of all the teams in the National Football League, the cities where they were located, and their best players, which gave him, even as a young boy, an excellent grasp of domestic geography.

When he was four years old, I enrolled him in a cooperative nursery. He enjoyed the group and made friends there. His favorite was a little boy named Andrew. At home we found a children's book, titled *Nobody Listens to Andrew,* about a boy who finds a bear in the house, but nobody in his family believes him or even has time to listen. Finally, Andrew shouts out the news loud enough his family gets the message.

Jeffrey really liked the book, and we read it to him a lot. Then one night, unexpectedly, Jeffrey said to Jamie and me, "Would you like me to read the book to you?" We were astounded. Jeffrey read every word of it to us. We assumed he had memorized it, but from then on, he loved to read any book he could find!

14

RESEARCH NOTES ON DEPRESSION AND CHILD SEXUAL ABUSE

In my research I have discovered there are numerous studies indicating a link between childhood sexual abuse (CSA) and depression.[41] Hall and Hall, a counselor and social worker, for example, have concluded that, among all the symptoms survivors experience, "depression has been found to be the most common long-term symptom."[42]

A New York psychologist researcher reported that "in almost every case of significant adult depression, some form of abuse was experienced in childhood, either physical, sexual, emotional, or, often, a combination."[43] While depression is important, it is not definitive in diagnosing CSA. Other authors agree, noting "… the absence of any specific syndrome in children who have been sexually abused …"[44] Canadian researchers in 2000 began their paper with the following: "There is strong evidence a history of childhood sexual abuse (CSA) is associated with adult depression."[45]

And in Duncan's book, *Healing from the Trauma of Childhood Sexual Abuse*, she observed depression often begins at the time of the abuse, as the child responds to the perpetrator's actions with a "sense of hopelessness and helplessness." And, Duncan adds, "If they try to suppress the memories ... depression returns."[46] Both boys and girls who have been sexually abused are at increased risk for the development of depression, and the risk continues into adulthood.

The list continues. A study reported in the *British Medical Journal* concluded women who were sexually abused were prone to depression as adults"[47] while a large and nationally (U.S.) representative study depicted the association of chronic depressive disorders in adults with childhood sexual abuse.[48]

Other studies, including those of Hartman and colleagues, reported survivors may have "difficulty in externalizing the abuse," which would result in their "thinking negatively about themselves."[49] "After years of negative self-thoughts, survivors had feelings of worthlessness and avoided others because they believed they had nothing to offer."[50] Ratican describes the survivor's depressed feelings to include "feeling down much of the time, having suicidal ideation [thoughts], having disturbed sleeping patterns, and having disturbed eating patterns."[51]

In my life I exhibited both disturbed sleeping and eating patterns when the kids were home, as I stayed up very late, losing sleep, and daily eating just one meal at night after everybody else was asleep.

In Duncan's book she continues, noting "depression involves thoughts, physical symptoms, behaviors, and feelings." She then defines how each of these areas is affected. The victim's thoughts may encompass a "lack of self-confidence" and a "negative view of the world ... Physical symptoms [in depression] can include lack of energy, tiredness and fatigue ... problems with not sleeping or with sleeping too much, and weight gain or loss ... Depressive feelings include hopelessness, discouragement, despair, fear, guilt, shame ... Behaviors related to depression include inactivity, sluggishness ... restlessness ... withdrawal, and dependency."[52]

"The long-term effects of childhood sexual abuse can be summarized as decreased energy, as well as a decrease in the zest for life, belief in self, and trust in the world." Duncan observes "each time their [survivors'] boundaries were violated, they felt anger. After years of suppression, a child's anger can turn into adult outrage."[53]

I'm sure for much of my life I was angry, although I didn't recognize it at the time. But I think the anorexia was inspired by unrecognized anger at my father.

It is known anger, which is turned inward, becomes depression.

Clinical psychologist, Tony Bates notes that depression provokes in survivors a "withdrawal from others and a turning against oneself." They are left with the conviction "they themselves are losers."[54]

15

JUMP INTO MY BED

*Cole and Putnam (1992) note that "survivors rely heavily on 'relatively immature coping strategies, which ... increase the likelihood of acting impulsively when frustrated, depressed, or anxious by (... engaging in misconduct such as substance abuse, **sexual acting out**, running away, and other self-destructive behaviors)."*[55]

I was deeply troubled by Rachel's illness on top of Jeffrey's bronchitis. They reminded me how fragile children can be, which frightened me. The fear may have been partly responsible for what happened next.

I had an affair, which I could never explain. I know many people have affairs, but mine was hard to understand. I was not unhappy in my marriage. I wasn't unfulfilled sexually. Jamie and I had a good relationship. We were well-matched in many ways and happy together.

I have an earlier example of sexual acting out, which may have been a prequel to the affair. Shortly after Maria's birth, I was enrolled in night school and had signed up for a geology class. I found the geology instructor appealing and had a fleeting thought one night of trying to seduce him. I actually visited him in his office, but since I had no intention of orchestrating a seduction, nothing happened. I then went home and told Jamie about it. We talked briefly, which is all it took.

I want to emphasize I've never approved of extra-marital affairs. I never intended to have one, and I am still ashamed of it. It is the most hurtful thing I have ever done, betraying my husband, my "knight in shining armor."

About a year before the affair, our friends Vicki and Jack, with whom we did the babysitting exchange, went for a bicycle ride with Jamie and me. I had a baby seat on the back of my bike for Maria, and Jack had one for Sandy, their daughter. We rode for a while until we reached a small pond where we stopped to rest. I was pregnant with Jeffrey at the time, and I was warm from the exertion of riding and pulling Maria's weight in addition to my own. "I want to jump in the pond to cool off," I said. Jamie, the voice of reason, objected while Jack encouraged me to do what felt good.

I listened to Jamie. He was right, of course. If I was wet as I rode back, I would get cold from the wind. But Jack's statement stuck with me. He seemed to be saying to do what *feels good*. I internalized his statement about self-actualization, which refers to "the full development of one's potential."

It wasn't until a year later, when Jeffrey was sick—coughing all day and night—I started thinking about how I could escape the sound. It seemed to me I was getting tired of my daily responsibilities, especially stressful ones, and I might have wanted some relief.

I was feeling both powerless and angry because Jamie and I had faithfully taken Jeffrey to doctors, and they seemed singularly unable to cure him. Daily we were giving him a prescribed medication, which he hated, and it seemed completely ineffective. I found it extremely frustrating to have to listen to him cough while I could do nothing to help him.

The anger I felt and the fear about Jeffrey's health inspired the activation of my subcortical brain region, causing my primitive brain to simply overwhelm my thinking brain.

At the time, Jamie was doing laboratory experiments at Walter Reed. He often came home for dinner, turned right around, and went back to work, which was very hard on me. Consequently, I would be alone with Jeffrey's coughing at night after I had listened to it all day.

I was very anxious about Jeffrey and began calling our friend Jack at night, who was at the time separated from Vicki. Our conversations went on for the better part of three months. Jamie was aware of these talks but did not give them much thought.

I don't remember what Jack and I talked about, but I know it wasn't personal. There were many things I never knew about him, such as his favorite foods, movies, music, or friends.

I guess he and I talked about psychology in general, but especially self-actualization, which fascinated me. Jack had a dream of becoming a psychiatrist, and I suspect our conversations may have mirrored his view of himself as a doctor helping a patient. Before it ever occurred to me as a possibility, I was becoming emotionally involved with Jack. It started creeping into our relationship.

When I learned Jack liked the poem "The Ballad of Sam McGee," I copied it onto a bed sheet and sent it to him for his birthday. When Jack told his psychiatrist about the gift, the doctor told him it implied I wanted to sleep with him.

Events snowballed soon after. Jack came to the house one day, knowing Jamie would be at work, and I started wondering if he had an interest in me too. Was Jack as guilty as I in orchestrating the affair? Was his visit a way of letting me know he was available? I think Jack may have had his own agenda. It seemed to me Jack had progressed from telling me to "jump in the pond" to suggesting I "jump into his bed."

Finally I felt impelled to take some kind of action. It appears my lower, or emotional, brain made the unfortunate decision to pursue a sexual liaison with a male friend. Unfortunately my lower brain had no direct access to my deep-seated, and very real, objections to extra-marital sexual coupling, which were stored in the thinking part of my brain.

Psychiatry Professors John Briere and Diana Elliot's study provide some basis for my actions. They note that "indiscriminate sexual activity by some sexual abuse survivors may provide distraction and avoidance of distress ..."[56]

Since this is what I sought at the time, I decided to act. A day or two after Mother's Day, I went to Jack's apartment and told him I wanted to have sex with him. This was my lower or emotional brain speaking, which meant I never considered talking to Jack about using protection, nor did I ask him about his recent sexual history.

If we were going to proceed, Jack decided he should call Jamie first to get his approval. I thought Jamie would simply say no, which would be the end of it; but Jamie was enough caught off guard he was thunderstruck. He told Jack we might as well go ahead with it. Jamie says now he thought I had given my heart to Jack. Therefore, he didn't think saying "no" would make much difference in the outcome. His thoughts were conditioned by his belief I would never have extramarital sex with someone I did not fully love.

Jamie's behavior can be further explained by what was going on in his brain. When faced with a traumatic situation like this, the upper brain centers go "offline" or, in other words, the thinking part of the brain becomes paralyzed, unable to process information.[57] Thus, when Jack made his call, Jamie was unable to deal adequately with his message and simply acquiesced to my desire to have sex. It was an unusual abandonment of his usual caretaker role; in essence he left me on my own.

Jamie told me later he no longer knew who I was. For years he has struggled with trying to understand how I could sexually betray the one person who had loved and cared for me all these years, always wanting the best for me. And I coupled with a friend I clearly did not love, and with whom I ended the relationship almost immediately thereafter.

I wish my thinking brain had been in control right then, and I could've actually thought about Jamie and what I was doing. I knew he would be terribly hurt by my action. But it was unfortunately the powerful emotional brain in control because, with the thinking brain, I never would have *chosen* to hurt Jamie the way I did.

But I was on auto-pilot, and my compulsion had a momentum propelling me into Jack's bedroom. The sex was as satisfying as it can be between friends. I found it difficult to be lustful or passionate, though. In fact, for me, the act itself and the afterglow were colored by the fact Jamie was aware of our coupling. Immediately after, the compulsion to have sex with Jack completely evaporated.

Jack and I talked afterward. He told me Jamie might want to have sex with me when I arrived home. I wondered if it was Jack's reaction to Vicki when she had sexual liaisons. It was definitely not Jamie's reaction.

I got dressed and headed home, and when I walked up the stairs to Jamie's and my bedroom afterward, we talked very little. As I climbed into bed with Jamie, I began—with my thinking brain again in charge—to realize the enormity of what I had done.

The next day, Jamie left for a couple of days to be with his parents. When he returned, he grabbed a few of his things and moved in with a friend. For a long time he came over after work, and we sat and talked about what had happened while sipping claret lemonades.

It was all talk, though. *Neither Jamie nor I dealt with our feelings. We successfully put them away to allow us to get on with the business of being a family. We agreed, of course, that no extramarital activities would be allowed in the future, but, of course, they were never supposed to occur in the first place.*

My affair did not fit the mold for most affairs. Our telephone conversations were about ordinary things. We never kissed or held hands or engaged in any sexual foreplay. Basically, Jack and I had a friendship which I, unfortunately, turned into something else.

I was very upset because I had acted against my deeply held moral creeds, and I knew I had grievously hurt Jamie. It was obvious he was in anguish, and I felt terrible about what I had done. Jamie had always loved me, always been good to me; and I had betrayed him and the trust he had in me. I found myself facing a shattered marriage, and I started cycling through it in my mind over and over, wondering how I could have been as unthinking and uncaring as I demonstrated. Unfortunately I didn't have an answer.

Jamie told me once I had acted against him just as my father had done to me, which hit me like nothing else he could have said. My betrayal was just like my father's betrayal of me.

I disapproved of my behavior. It was strictly against my belief system as well as my mental picture of who I was. Yet, despite that, I did it. It makes me wonder what force or motivation was compelling enough as to make me act against my self-interest. A friend told me of a name for the condition. It is called cognitive dissonance. It means just what I said, that my behavior was inconsistent with my belief system.

After this night, I only saw Jack briefly one more time as it was time to end the relationship. Clearly Jamie would have no more of this type of behavior if our marriage was to remain viable, and when Jamie met with Jack a week or two later, it was evident Jack had absolutely no interest in continuing to see or talk to me. For me, I had decided immediately after the affair, that sex with Jack was not what I needed. After saying good-bye to Jack, I never called him again and did not see him until many years later at his daughter's wedding.

Jamie came very close to leaving me, and his love for me never fully recovered. He didn't trust me around men again. For decades, the affair shattered what he thought our relationship entailed. It was, for him, a permanent wound he put away, at least for a considerable time. During the remainder of May and well into June, the brief affair and its consequences gradually faded from our lives.

What our discussions lacked back then was any insight into what had been going on with me or why I had perpetuated the one-night stand. We had no resources available to us to even begin to comprehend the dynamics at play.

In time Jamie came to the conclusion, which I had known from the beginning, he was never in competition with Jack for my affection. I tried to emphasize to Jamie my interest in Jack had not really been about sex, nor was it fueled by romantic desire or eroticism. No, it was conditions at home causing my emotional brain to be in control. I never would have had an affair if my thinking brain had been fully operative; no, I would have realized my thinking was muddled, and I had confused what I wanted from what I needed, which, I learned, is a sequela of sexual abuse.[58] I thought I *wanted* a distraction from Jeffrey's coughing, and a sense of control, which I would accomplish by having sex with Jack. But what I needed was not a distraction, but to ask Jamie for what I needed, which was for him to stay home some nights to support me while Jeffrey coughed. Even more, I needed for Jamie and me together to search for a new doctor for Jeffrey.

16

NOW WE ARE COMPLETE

I became pregnant again when Jeffrey was one and a half. I have wondered if I decided to have a third child because of Jeffrey's illness. I think my unconscious mind was still desperately afraid of losing my little baby.

I enjoyed my home birth tremendously and decided to repeat the experience.

One morning close to my due date for our third child, we took Maria and Jeffrey shopping for film for Jamie's camera. When I told Jamie I felt funny, he replied, "You're in labor."

In the afternoon Jamie took Maria and Jeffrey to a friend's house, and my labor coach arrived. She checked my birthing status and smiled at me saying, "How would you like to have a baby in an hour?"

"An hour?" I asked, shocked. I didn't feel like I was in hard labor yet. Soon the rest of the crew arrived. There were three or four nurses in attendance. One was a nurse from the doctor's office; another was an obstetrics nurse from the hospital, who was ready to deliver the baby in case the doctor was delayed; and a third nurse seemed to be there by choice. She merely watched the birth, in tears because "it was beautiful."

When the doctor arrived, he and I worked as a team to deliver the baby. Jamie took pictures. Later he said I seemed to withdraw into myself during the delivery. I suspect it was because I was concentrating on what was going on inside my body. It made sense to me.

When Maria and Jeffrey came back to our house after the delivery, we all had dinner and went to bed. Rachel, our newborn, spent the first night in bed with Jamie and me, nestled between the two of us. She never woke up or cried. The next morning we awoke, and Maria and Jeffrey climbed in bed with us and the new baby. It was a wonderful moment of togetherness. We bonded as a whole family, the newest member included.

Not only was Rachel an easy baby, but she continued to be easy, even as she grew older. It was as if she understood she was the latest addition to our family, and it was her job to fit into the pre-existing group—at mealtimes and at bedtimes—and she did!

I remember one time when she was very young, she came to me and asked if I had any gum. I often bought some for her and her brother and kept it in my purse. I told her to look in there, and she found two pieces, one red and one green. Rachel immediately took both pieces to Jeffrey and offered them to him before she made her own choice. "Which one do you want, Seh-she?" she asked. This was her pronunciation of Jeffrey's name.

I thought it was very sweet she thought about her brother first, even at a very young age.

She was a much healthier infant than Jeffrey, but when she was three, she caught cold one day and became increasingly sick as the night progressed. Sometime late she called out to me, and I went in to check on her. As she was burning up with fever, I immediately ran a cold bath and immersed her. When I thought she was cooler, I put her back in bed and said good night, but suddenly she began talking to me. "Look, there's a rabbit up there, Mommy."

"Okay," I said; "but it's time for you to go back to sleep." "There's a giraffe," she said, "and monkeys, and they're jumping."

Suddenly, my heart almost stopped. I realized Rachel was actually seeing these animals. She was hallucinating. We rushed her to the hospital, and the nurse grabbed her out of my arms and disappeared with her. The hospital wanted me to sign her in, but I couldn't stand there and answer questions calmly right then; instead I tried one door in the emergency room and then the next until I discovered where she was. The nurses had put her into a tub of water. I watched as they added ice cubes. They kept her there until her temperature was down from 106 to 103 degrees. The danger was past, but I remember how nervous I was when they released her, thinking they should keep her until her temperature was back to normal. However, she recovered nicely afterward.

As Rachel grew older, I used to talk to her about her hallucinations with the animals. I was afraid the scary event would get buried somewhere in her unconscious, and she would later be afraid of something without knowing what it was or why.

I was relieved to be able to help Rachel then. Many, many nights I had felt helpless with Jeffrey, but at least I was able to do something to make my youngest child feel better. Thank goodness!

17

1973: RUNNING AWAY

"Impulsive behavior includes a history of running away ..."[59]

I was unhappy in Silver Spring, a suburb of Washington, D.C. It took me a long time to become really aware of the fact I hated living there. There were just too many cars, too much cement, and too many people. The worst part was going to the local market where the aisles were too small, and shoppers repeatedly bumped my cart. There was no room to maneuver. I missed the open spaces dreadfully. I spent the latter part of my childhood in a small village. I was used to having room to move around, to breathe. I felt stifled and unhappy.

I didn't share my growing dislike of the area with Jamie. It seemed he and I never talked about things, important or not. I just came up with a quick plan for the children and me to leave the suburbs and for Jamie to follow us later.

Here was a perfect example of my impulsivity. In three days' time I not only decided to go to nursing school, but I found an LPN (licensed practical nursing) program in upstate New York, which agreed to admit me immediately. I asked a young friend who was between jobs if she was willing to go to Malone, New York, with me to babysit my three kids for a year. Then I kissed Jamie goodbye, put Jeffrey and Rachel in the car—Maria and Jamie were to follow soon after—and headed north without a backward glance. I didn't consider how it would feel for Jamie or for the kids to be uprooted. Jamie was left alone to fix up and sell the house. I was on a mission to move us out of suburbia. I don't think Jamie was too happy about my plan, but he was always very supportive of me.

I picked up Margot, the babysitter, on the way and drove endlessly in our VW station wagon, as Malone is at the roof of New York State. I remember how disappointed I was Malone isn't located in the beautiful Adirondack Mountains but north of them.

We found a passable apartment and began to settle in. Since there was no refrigerator, we bought a small "ice box," which we literally kept cool with blocks of ice. And as there was only one bedroom, we all slept on mattresses on the floor.

Within a day or two, Jamie arrived with Maria and the furniture. He left them with me and headed back to Silver Spring. He was going to finish up his job at Walter Reed and join us sometime in the future.

On Monday morning, only three days after we arrived, the truancy officer paid me a visit.

He informed me that it was his understanding I had moved in with children, and they were required to be in school. I went and signed them up; then I started my nursing classes. Our life in Malone began in earnest.

I enjoyed being a student again. My lessons about diseases in the body and the accompanying treatments were interesting. Studying the structure of the body and the physiology was more challenging, but we were allowed to progress at our own rate and take an individual test at the end of each chapter. The best part of the nursing program was our time in the hospital. We had rounds in surgery, pediatrics, obstetrics, and the nursing home. I loved obstetrics and was thrilled to be able to observe a Caesarean birth. I would don my white uniform and my pert white cap, and I not only looked the part, but I actually started to feel like a nurse. The feeling it gave me made me think I had made a good choice.

Our favorite pastime was taking trips north on the weekends. Crossing the American-Canadian border could be tricky. We were in

Malone in 1973 during the Vietnam War, and I guess the border patrol was on increased lookout for men avoiding the draft by traveling north.

There was one time when I was in potentially serious trouble with the border patrol, and it was my own fault. On one of our weekend trips back to the U.S. from Canada, I found a new route on a little-traveled highway to take us home. It turned out the border station on this road was closed, according to the sign, but there was no barrier blocking traffic. The sign said anybody crossing when the station was closed should proceed back to an open border station as soon as possible. I drove on across the border. As I went past a crossroad, a U.S. border patrol officer was traveling east to west. He saw me, turned around, came back, and stopped me.

"Where are you going?" he asked me. "Malone," I answered. He said, "Follow me." Now if I had thought more quickly, I would have immediately realized the answer he was looking for was my intention to go back to the border station that was open.

I could have avoided all the following problems if I had been more careful in my response. I followed him back to the open border station where he told me I had crossed the border illegally, and the fine was $2100. I was aghast! "I don't have $2100," I said, with all the bravado I could muster. "Well, I can reduce the fine to $100," he noted. I guess I was supposed to be incredibly grateful, but I didn't even have $100 in the bank at that particular time, which I told him. But it was apparently too much for him. He told me he would have to impound the car and the contents—a few small things we had bought in Canada—until I could find the money. In the meantime, he drove us the twelve miles back to Malone.

It's not clear why I ignored the sign, but I believe it had something to do with what I learned about rules as I was growing up with my parents. For my mother, breaking rules was usually due to her excessive drinking. There was one time, for instance, when we were all at a party at my in-laws' place. My mom had too much to drink and managed to shed both her skirt and her wig before she left the scene.

On another occasion she was driving from New York City and did a U-turn on the George Washington Bridge just prior to the toll booths. This is extremely dangerous, which the policeman who stopped her told her. Amazingly enough, he didn't even give her a warning, though!

Once the border patrol had driven us home, I called Jamie. He and I had arranged to talk for at least one minute at 11 p.m. each evening during our separation. This time I had a wild story to tell him. He wired me the money, and the next day a friend drove me back out to the border station to retrieve my car.

I missed Jamie. We didn't see him again until Christmas. He and I decided we would meet at his parents' house in Bronxville, and then drive back together to our home in Silver Spring, Maryland, where we would spend Christmas. We decided to set it up as a surprise for the kids.

Our drive was intense as we set out. We got on the Northway (I-87) in the middle of a blizzard. It was difficult driving, but I had the advantage of being the only car on the road. Nobody else dared to venture out during the storm. It was another risky choice, but I was at least glad I didn't have to worry about skidding into anybody as we progressed about 150 miles south. We stopped off in Schenectady on our way to stay with my parents for a night. My relationship with them had been less tumultuous since I had gotten married, and I liked giving my kids the opportunity to get to see their grandparents. We spent a quiet evening in, glad to be shielded from the winter storm. The next morning my father pulled out a warm water hose to melt the ice on the wheels before we could get back on the road.

When we arrived at Jamie's parents' house in Bronxville, his mother told the kids to go upstairs. Up they went, and I soon heard their cries of joy as they saw their father again. After a couple of days, we all piled in the car and headed south once more, back to Silver Spring.

We spent a lovely Christmas in our old house, our last Christmas there. It was sad saying goodbye to the house, but we did leave a plaque in the closet of the bedroom where Rachel was born. It read, "In this room Rachel Montgomery drew her first breath of life." I wonder if it is still there.

After seeing Jamie at Christmas, it was difficult to leave him again and return to Malone. I realized suddenly how much I had been missing him. Even as busy as I was, spring seemed like such a long time away. I had to remind myself it was I who had undertaken the move out of Silver Spring with little thought of how it would feel down the line. It was another example of my impulsiveness overwhelming my examination of the consequences.

As soon as Jamie re-joined us, everything snapped back into place, but the weeks leading up to his arrival had been rough. I decided to get a puppy for the children, and we all went to the pound and picked one out. The kids named her Smokey Malone Pup. She was not trained, which was problematic at best, but when we finally managed the training, she became a wonderful family pet.

Unfortunately, I didn't realize we needed to get Smokey spayed. When she went into heat, it seemed like every male dog for miles around was attracted to Smokey. Dogs would hang around our front porch, trying to get close to her. I got a ticket for disturbing the peace. None of the owners of the male dogs received any kind of citation or warning. As I wanted to protest the unfairness, I put a leash on Smokey; the kids and I then walked the two blocks to the police station as at least twenty male dogs followed us. We made quite a procession! When I opened the door to the station with my dog and the others in tow, a policeman came to the head of the stairs on the second floor. He was angry enough his face turned purple as he ordered us to leave.

The next day Jamie arrived to save the day. He put Smokey in his car, and we all piled in. He rolled the windows down and drove slowly out of town. The male dogs followed us for miles but gradually dropped off until all of them were gone.

When he re-joined us, it felt like I had completed an experiment in living without Jamie. What I concluded was life was much more chaotic when we were apart. I was more impulsive as well as reactive to outside events. One of Jamie's primary effects on the family has been stability, which was largely missing in Malone. He was always careful about making plans and carrying them out. He sees the big picture; these traits make life a great deal calmer.

Slowly I realized I had again confused what I wanted and what I needed. I *wanted* a nursing degree because I thought if I had a job to help support us, it would enable us to leave Silver Spring. But I gradually became aware that my year separating the family from Jamie—and the expense of us living apart—had been unnecessary. I had simply had to have a conversation with Jamie about my need to leave Silver Spring.

18

AN UNEXPECTED
RESPITE

After my nursing program ended, we made a decision to leave Malone and eventually ended up in the Washington, D.C., area. We wanted to live outside the metropolitan area and settled on Haymarket, Virginia, about 40 miles west of D.C. We purchased a home; it was a modest place about seven miles from the center of town at the base of the local mountain range.

I drove around the place at night, and it felt very dark and spooky to me. It was too much for me, and I decided I wanted to leave. I was about to break the news to Jamie that I wasn't happy there, but something clicked for me at the end of a year. I don't know what it was, but my restless feeling passed. I had calmed down. I liked the house, and it became our home. We stayed in the house for twenty-one years. It is the house where the children grew up and left home … and where Jeffrey died.

It was a comfortable house for all of us. However, the school system was a huge concern. The elementary school was in a rural area, and it wasn't as good as the kids' schools had been in either Silver Spring or Malone.

I put up with it a couple of years; then I came up with a unique solution to overcome the problems—I would teach the kids at home. However, I understood there were, at the time, significant legal issues associated with home schooling. My solution was to write the American Civil Liberties Union (ACLU) for help. One of their lawyers agreed to contact the school system for me. The county administration's clever response was to assign me the title of Collegiate Teacher; thus, I became legitimate in their eyes.

Very few people were home schooling in 1978. Yet it was one of the happiest experiences of my life! My kids were bright and eager to learn. We lived near the District of Columbia and visited the museums there. The BBC decided to televise all of Shakespeare's plays, and we often curled up and watched them. I discovered the science of ecology, and we visited a nearby pond to study its biosystem. There was a German lady nearby who taught Jeffrey the language. And Rachel did gymnastics, and Jeffrey played soccer.

I home-schooled the kids for four years, all during middle school. It was a big adjustment for all of us when they re-entered the school system. I loved having them at home, "teaching" them, and doing activities together.

When the kids re-entered school, I was depressed and sat around and moped for months. I finally realized I needed to get out of the house and find something to do. Happily for me, a teacher at the private school, where Jeffrey had begun ninth grade, had left suddenly; and the headmaster asked me if I would like to fill his position. I was delighted!

PART

3 TRAUMA RETURNS

Clearly the first half of my life was a combination of healthy and unhealthy forces. Certainly falling in love with Jamie, marrying him, and together raising three beautiful children were wholesome behaviors. And it was pure joy when I was able to teach two of my children at home.

But there were unwholesome behaviors at work at the same time. Whether I was a child suffering sexual abuse or starving myself or battling depression, running away to the wilds of New York State, or breaking my husband's heart, I was clearly a troubled soul. And perhaps the sum of all my unhealthy behavior contributed to the worst loss of all, which was the devastating suicide of our sixteen-year-old son. Grieving the loss threw us into despair; I had never come as close to giving up. My family and my therapist were crucial to my survival.

I found the therapist prepared to help me work through the feelings associated with child sexual abuse as well. These feelings, generated years earlier, had never been addressed or resolved; and her work in this area was critical. My son's death, and the work I did in therapy, turned out to be the turning point of my life.

But time moved on, and there was other business simmering in the background. Consider the affair, for instance. Jamie and I had made a conscious decision to put the event away, allowing us to get on with the business of raising a family. It worked well for many years for both of us.

But nature had other plans. Both Jamie, with the affair, and I, with the sexual abuse, separately experienced flashbacks, which refers to the occurrence of feelings in the present relating to an experience from the past. Part 3 is the story of the resurfacing of both of these traumas and the additional work we did toward healing.

I was well into the healing process when I learned that whether I was holding my minister responsible for his inappropriate behavior or setting boundaries where necessary, I could do what I needed to do.

19

THE END OF LIFE
AS WE KNEW IT

*"... almost all of the [suicide] deaths occurred at home
... maybe it was an impulsive act..."*[60]

Since Jeffrey and I were finished with classes early, I arranged for us to meet in the parking lot to begin our hour-long drive home. We left Rachel there to finish her classes.

He was in his junior year at a private school and seemed reasonably comfortable there. He was very excited when he first started ninth grade after being homeschooled much of his life. Now he seemed disengaged from his academic life. I suspected it was a combination of the newness wearing off and normal teenage angst. He was not athletic, but he had become a leader of the marching band. It seemed to me he had carved out a niche for himself.

Jeffrey and I climbed in the car and wended our way homeward. He told me about his classes as I drove and then said, "Since I don't have any homework, can I watch TV when we get home?"

"Uh-uh," I responded, shaking my head. "I need the TV room as my friend Alice will be visiting." Alice was a seminarian at our church, studying for the ministry. I was on a committee, which met with her monthly. We had become good friends.

A couple of hours later, after some tea and conversation, Alice took her leave. It was time for me to drive the seven miles to our local town to pick Rachel up from the school bus stop.

I passed by Jeffrey on my way out the door. He had been on the living room couch reading all afternoon. I invited him to ride with me.

"No, thanks," he said. "In fact," he continued, "I was five minutes from killing myself, and you didn't even know it."

I stopped and looked at Jeffrey for a long moment. I couldn't believe his words. I didn't hear them for what they were. I heard anger; it never occurred to me they were a plea for help.

"What are you angry about, the TV?" I asked. He didn't answer, and I continued, "Come with me, Jeffrey, and we can talk about whatever is bothering you."

"No," he responded. "Thank you. I'd rather not."

"Please," I said. "It would give us a chance to talk. I need to talk to you." As Jeffrey resisted, I was afraid of being late for my daughter and left.

I drove to town and picked Rachel up, taking a minute to say hello to my friend Audrey before we drove home. As we turned into the driveway, Rachel's face became burned into my memory. It was a look of horror, such that I had never seen before.

I followed her eyes until I, too, saw my son hanging from a tree in our backyard.

At the moment, there was no other adult in sight. I had to be in charge. I told Rachel to dial 911, and I started doing CPR. Within a few minutes, Jamie came home from work, the emergency vehicles trailing right behind him.

Jeffrey was suddenly out of our hands. A helicopter flew him to the Children's Hospital in Washington, D.C. When Jeffrey arrived, he was connected to life support in the ICU. The doctor told us the medications they were using were much too strong for Jeffrey's heart. They would not be effective long-term.

Maria, our eldest daughter, and her boyfriend flew in from Florida where they went to school. Jamie's father came in from New York. We all slept as well as we could on the chairs and couches in the waiting room.

Late the next day the doctor came to speak to us again, suggesting, as night was approaching, we consider taking Jeffrey off life support. "It is only a matter of time before it will no longer be able to fulfill its function."

We took his advice. We all gathered around Jeffrey's bed, holding hands, tears running down our cheeks. One by one we said goodbye, and we disconnected the life support.

I managed to put myself on autopilot. We did what we needed to do. Jamie and I went to the morgue to identify Jeffrey's body. Then we visited Charlie, our minister, to make arrangements for the funeral.

The ceremony was held on a cold day in mid-March. Wakefield School sent a busload of students to attend. The minister told a lovely story about a caterpillar crawling across a Persian rug of many colors. Sometimes he was sad (blue), sometimes angry (red), or envious (green). He couldn't make sense of the colors, but his perspective improved when he became a butterfly and flew over the Oriental rug and saw the gorgeous pattern woven into it.

Three days later I visited Wakefield School and told the students gathered there Jeffrey had made a terrible mistake, which I strongly believed. As I struggled to find my way through the awful grief, I was also faced with my guilt and my depression. Why hadn't I just stayed home? My decision, my lack of judgment, many times had I desperately tried to change them in my mind.

I slowly realized I could not by myself fight the terrible depression threatening to overcome me. I had always told myself I would die if one of my children died. And faced with the situation, I wanted nothing more than to give up, to stop trying, to give in to the grief. Had I had only the one child, it would have been my answer. But I still had two girls who were alive, one of them still at home. She and her brother were the ones I had home schooled, and we three had been very close. If I loved Rachel, how could I burden her with my death on top of her brother's? I loved her too much to do this to her, as I had no idea how she would handle all the grief.

I knew I needed help. I was not at all sure how much time I would have before the terrible grief would drag me down beyond recall. I checked around until I found a psychotherapist who was available, and I started counseling with her. I discovered there was no blame in therapy, which felt like a gift. I found it was a relief to talk about Jeffrey without experiencing any judgment, for I was already judging myself harshly.

Therapy was a slow process; the grief was very deep. At the same time we started a small grief group at church with our beloved minister, Charlie. There, we were surrounded by people who were grieving, which made us comfortable enough we could share our daily struggles with the other members.

At home we made a few small changes to try to make Jeffrey's absence less obvious. We ate meals in the sun room, for instance, instead of around the dining room table, and we invited our friend Pat to join us at dinner time. Her family had moved; as Pat had been left behind to sell their house, she was alone and available to join us.

Rachel went to school on her birthday, and I went on to work. Once there I talked to a friend, who suggested the birthday must be a happy occasion. I said, "No ... because it was Rachel's first birthday without Jeffrey, and for the first time she was the same age as Jeffrey." Once the friend heard what I said, she sent Rachel a beautiful "sweet sixteen" bouquet. In the evening we celebrated in the park instead of at home. And afterward, Rachel left us and went to a basketball game with her friends.

A year later Rachel went to college, which was fortunately not too far from home, so we did not feel we had *lost* her. I remember we drove down to see her one time, not realizing how she was feeling after a fight with her boyfriend. Very upset, she was in bed with the blinds drawn. Poor Rachel! After my recent loss, I reacted badly when I saw her. I hurriedly put the blinds up and yanked her out of bed. As unreasonable as I was, I believe Rachel understood perfectly. Not only did she miss Jeffrey herself, but she was well aware of my loss.

Before Rachel left home, there were a great many Sundays when Rachel and I (who never fought) would argue about something stupid, like who had lost more. Then we would dissolve into tears. It was a terrible time, which seemed to go on forever.

20

1985: FALLOUT

"Maladaptive boundaries are a crippling long-term consequence of abuse."[61]

Several months after Jeffrey's death, I was still feeling terribly sad. Jeffrey had told me he was on the verge of killing himself, but I didn't think he meant it. The thought haunted me. I certainly did not recognize the risk was real—it seems I have always misinterpreted or under-estimated risk.

I wished I could go back. My brain was awake and alert now, but it wasn't possible. How often it seems we never get a second chance. No, but at least I had found a therapist who was with me for the duration, helping me find my way through the terrible pain, and, as noted, we had joined a grief group at church. In addition to those, Jamie and I discovered a national group for bereaved parents, Compassionate Friends. We attended monthly meetings for a long time. Certainly the therapist and the support groups were immensely helpful during my long struggle out of the abyss.

Sometime later I realized that, of all the feelings Jeffrey's suicide brought up, one of them was anger because of the choice he made. Didn't he know we were ready to give him whatever help he needed? He never asked or gave us a chance.

Since I couldn't admit to myself that I was angry at Jeffrey for what he had done, my anger surfaced in other situations. I believe it caused me to start taking more personal risks—ignoring boundaries, for instance. I mention this because I became involved in a couple of relationships with men where boundaries became blurred. The timing would seem to indicate Jeffrey's death triggered some of the negative coping strategies I had adopted from my childhood trauma. My ability to establish and maintain my role in relationships was shaken.

One involved the chaplain at Children's Hospital where Jeffrey was treated. A nurse asked me if I wanted to talk to him. When Tim came in, he spent the better part of the day with me, not saying much but sitting quietly with me in my grief. I was glad for his presence, asking nothing of him.

A couple of days after we left the hospital, Tim called me at home to invite me to visit a pet store with him to see the puppies, which is when he started to ignore his role as hospital chaplain. I was sure he just felt sorry for me and was trying to extend his hand in friendship.

I was not strong enough to say, "Excuse me, but this is inappropriate. You belong in the hospital with the people there." Because the hand of friendship felt good, I unfortunately began ignoring boundaries myself, and my vulnerability sabotaged me.

We started talking on the phone frequently. I was hurting too much to realize I had become emotionally involved. All of a sudden, I found myself envisioning running away to a mountaintop with him as I tried to escape the pain, the grief.

It reminded me of something. I used to say to Jamie I could have been a nun or a whore. The whore is about being angry, of course, but the option of becoming a nun represented to me a retreat from the world. I suspect—because of Tim's affiliation with the church—I thought about him in terms of escape. It may be what I was referring to by my escape to the mountaintop.

I realized, though, that Tim had ignored the limits of his role as hospital chaplain. He soon decided to leave the seminary and start studying social work; then he moved back home to Oregon. We wrote back and forth for some time, but I stopped when Jamie and my therapist objected.

I'm glad I did though. I questioned Tim's role in our friendship. What did he derive from it? Was he just sympathetic and trying to help me? Or was he complicit in fostering an emotional relationship for himself? Unfortunately, I will never be able to answer these questions, but I have realized Tim clearly ignored the confines of his role.

I myself wasn't always without guilt when it came to men. I began ignoring boundaries with my boss at work. I didn't go back to teaching after Jeffrey died. Instead I found an easy, mindless secretarial job in a rental office in downtown Washington, D.C.

My job helped me make money while still functioning at an elementary level. The ease of the job, I think, contributed to the development of my relationship with my boss, Chip, a very kind, understanding male. While working, I began to go through menopause early, but then I began spotting long after the time bleeding would be considered normal. The doctor did four biopsies to check for uterine cancer, and I had to call his office each time for the results. And the calls were made while I was at work. The calls made me so nervous I started talking to Chip about my bleeding problems, which was totally inappropriate.

I have since wondered why I didn't go to Jamie's office for lunch and make my calls to the doctor from there.

Jamie became upset at my new relationship, pointing out to me Wikipedia's definition of personal boundaries as the "guidelines, rules, and limits" a person creates to identify for himself "what are reasonable, safe, and permissible ways for others to behave around him." I understood and even agreed with him, and we decided to see a marriage counselor. She sided with Jamie, telling me I should quit my job and break off contact with Chip. She called it an unhealthy situation and quoted Erin Carpenter, who noted that "the tasks ... of keeping boundaries in relationships are difficult ... especially for those abused during childhood."[62]

In thinking about my behavior, I became aware of a possible reason for my over-involvement with males. A major issue operating under the surface all along involved my long-standing need for validation from men.

I remember feeling dirty or devalued as a result of the sexual abuse. Other men, with whom I could share intimacy, provided me with external acceptance, despite my diminished feeling inside. Their friendship validated my worthiness, or at least it was what I hoped. I think it was, in part, what I needed from Jack. Once I achieved the goal, it was relatively easy for me to give him up. I can't help wondering if the same issue was a significant factor in the recent story.

I believe the validation-seeking behavior was rekindled in me because, when I think about feeling devalued, I realize Jeffrey's death had made me feel diminished as a mother.

The marriage counselor told me how I "romanticize my relationships with men … ." By characterizing my behavior directly, she made me really aware of my actions, enabling me to confront and control them. This was the key, which finally allowed me to change the behavior. Jamie could validate me whenever I needed it.

As I learned to stop seeking validation from outside men, I gradually worked through the immense pain and sadness caused by Jeffrey's death. The grief certainly represented the biggest challenge of my life—to learn to live in a world without my beloved son.

21

A BOUNDARY
PROBLEM REVERSED

While we were struggling with our grief, Jamie and I turned to our church community for support and healing. Our minister Charlie met with us each week to check on how we were doing with our grief. In time, other grieving church members joined us. It was a safe space for all of us. We had the greatest respect for Charlie, both as an ordained minister and as a caring, insightful friend.

We were devastated when we learned Charlie had lung cancer. He had to stop hosting the group as his health deteriorated, and he passed away shortly after. He is sadly missed, but he is still near and dear to our hearts. He helped us in many, many ways.

When it came time to find a minister to fill Charlie's position, none of the candidates could fill his shoes. I was a member of the church Vestry, the group involved in the business of running the local church. It fell upon the other members and me to review the applications. We received a packet of information about Greg, one of the front runners. However, it included a message from our Bishop, noting that he had been accused of fostering inappropriate relations with women in his previous church. It was a red flag for me, but his name kept resurfacing in our discussions. The Vestry voted to accept Greg after I had gotten tired and left the meeting.

When I met him, he seemed genuinely nice, and I decided to give him a chance. I guess I knew there was a risk involved, but I have always considered ministers to be resources during times of trouble, and I was still struggling with Jeffrey's death. I decided to visit Greg for support at night after work.

I was alone in a room with Greg regularly, and nothing untoward happened for a long time. But one night he began to pray, as usual. He asked God to help me heal, and then said, "We must let Susan know we love her." Those words could have been innocent, but the room suddenly fell strangely quiet. He paused and looked at me before continuing, "No, I can't say this." I was anxious for him to get on with the prayer, but he just paused again. He stared at me before saying, "But, yes, I can say it, for I do love her."

I left his office as quickly as possible afterward. I was both anxious and angry, but I didn't know what to do. I continued to see Greg in his office a couple more times, but I didn't tell Jamie about what he said right away. I wanted to work out a game plan on my own.

Greg's statement caused me to pause. I certainly wasn't sexually or emotionally involved with him on any level, but there were enough red flags to make me consider canceling my meetings with him.

But I decided—perhaps foolishly—to give Greg one more chance. Maybe I wanted to prove to myself I was in control. Besides, I was still grieving, and I *wanted* to believe Greg could help me.

Finally he did cross a line in a way not even I could deny. Jamie and I went to a Christmas party at his house. I was wearing a red dress with my petticoat showing. It looked festive to me, and I decided not to worry about it. When we arrived, I went upstairs to the powder room, and as I made my way back down, Greg appeared at the bottom of the stairs.

I immediately felt the same strange silence I'd felt in his office. No other party goers were around.

"I was going to tell you your slip was showing," he said. "Then I realized you already knew it."

"You're right," I responded, laughing uncomfortably. "I did know it."

Then, without warning, he kissed me fully on the lips.

I was appalled. I didn't think anyone had seen the kiss, but the hubris behind it made me furious. He took liberties with me. I was upset, but I didn't tell Jamie for a long time. I was afraid of what he would do. I finally realized fully that Gregory had flagrantly overstepped his boundaries, and I needed to stop visiting him.

I couldn't get his actions out of my head. The more I thought about him, the more upset I got, and the more I thought of the other women he could victimize. Greg had been talking about moving on to another parish, and all of the innocent women at the new church were swimming through my mind as well.

This is why I decided to report Greg. I knew it would create serious problems for him, but the other women in the back of my head pushed me forward. I couldn't protect him and them at the same time, so it really wasn't a choice. I wasn't the first victim, and I knew I wouldn't be the last.

Months before Greg arrived, I had met our bishop and felt I could trust him. He had come to our church for a confirmation ceremony and had given a beautiful sermon about waiting for God to answer prayers and make things right. When I talked to him later about my son's death, he expressed his sorrow and demonstrated concern for me, even though it was the first and only time we met.

When I went to see the bishop, he listened to my story about Greg very carefully. He apologized on behalf of the church and offered me psychotherapy, but I told him I already had a therapist.

The hardest thing was my decision to tell Greg I had reported his behavior. The bishop told me I didn't have to talk to Greg directly, but I wanted to. I was very angry. Greg was improper in his behavior, and I wanted to hold him accountable.

I called Greg and set up a meeting at a local restaurant. I was very nervous. Part of me felt like I must be over-stepping my role because ministers are people with authority.

But then I remembered that Gregory—like my father—had taken advantage of his authority over me.

When I met up with him, this perspective helped me look him in the eye and say, "I have gone to see the Bishop and reported your behavior to him." He looked completely deflated, as if I had kicked him in the stomach. I might have felt sorry for him, but I was too angry, too determined. I was a woman on a mission.

Afterward I left.

Jamie and I had arranged to meet at the entrance to the restaurant, and as we drove away, I raised my fist in the air and yelled, "Yes!" I felt empowered, and I realized it was not only about Gregory.

No, I realize not many people get the opportunity to hold their abusers accountable, but we hope it is changing with the growing consciousness of women's issues.

In addition, my dad died long before I had the courage to confront him. I never again saw the man who dragged me and groped me in my sister's neighborhood. Now, finally, I had done with Greg what I couldn't do with either of them. I had held him accountable.

My experience with Greg provided me with a real learning opportunity. It was my father who destroyed my ability to forge boundaries, requiring me to test limits to try to find them. I finally established a hard boundary with Greg, and I did it by myself and for myself!

I saw Greg having to deal with the consequences of his actions. He was defrocked by the Bishop. He is no longer an ordained minister of the Episcopal Church, and I don't feel sorry about it. It is no more than he deserved. I have heard of eleven or twelve other women from my church, who came forward, reporting Greg had been inappropriate with them as well.

Thus I became the spokesperson for far more women than I realized, probably because Greg's actions represented much more to me than to the other women he approached.

Holding Greg accountable *felt* wonderful! I had finally learned I don't have to remain a victim, and I can hold abusers accountable, whether it's my minister, my father, or a complete stranger. My internal message declared I am a victim no more!

I finally stopped the behavior I had learned from the abuse experience. I no longer sexualized relationships or aligned myself with abusive men, which felt like closure to me.

22

RECURRENCE: TIME FOLDED BACK ON ITSELF

J amie decided to take early retirement, which inspired us to leave our long-time home in Haymarket and move to Virginia's Shenandoah Valley. We had been spending weekends in nearby Lexington, Virginia, for many months and bought an old farmhouse there—our retirement home.

Once there, we planned to take a trip north to New York State to visit our families. Jamie's father and two sisters lived in Bronxville; my mom was in Schenectady, and my sister's home was in the middle of the state, just west of Oneonta. Years ago we established a routine on these journeys. We parked our car in Bronxville, took the commuter line to Grand Central Station, walked to a Jewish delicatessen on Third Avenue where we ate, and then headed back to the suburb where his family lived. This year our trip was no different.

We were on the train when we reached the Botanical Gardens station; all of a sudden I felt as if I had been enveloped by a gaseous cloud. It wasn't anything visual, but it took over my senses. It filled me with the most awful feelings—terror, a sense of evil, anger, dread, sadness, and grief. I turned around in my seat to see if there was something to which

I could attach the feelings in order to explain them. There was nothing. I felt like I had been run over by a steam roller or hit by a ton of bricks.

When I could catch my breath on the train, I tried to tell Jamie about my experience, but it was hard to explain. I had a strange and eerie confrontation with a specter of feelings, but nothing in my day-to-day life could compare with it.

I wanted nothing more than to curl up in a ball with Jamie holding me tightly, but we weren't home. The flashback isolated me from Jamie's family, as well as my own, through the rest of the trip, just as the original sexual abuse had done. I hadn't told anybody about the abuse because I was ashamed. Even though there was no shame in the flashback, who could I tell beside Jamie? I suffered in silence and prayed for our visits to be over quickly.

Being terribly distressed by the event, which I did not understand, I later buried myself in books and research articles looking for answers. I also had a couple of phone conversations with my therapist. What I discovered is I had apparently had a "flashback" pertaining to the sexual abuse, but I had no idea why the feelings had come up at this particular time. In Karen Duncan's book on sexual abuse, she notes that "Flashbacks ... can occur rather suddenly and catch a woman off guard in a way, which is similar to how she felt when the perpetrator abused her."[63] Wendy Maltz would agree, noting that "flashbacks usually happen without warning."[64] Another quote from van der Kolk's book spoke to me when he talked about a flashback occurring "... as if time is folded or warped, making the past and present merge."[65]

Once we were home, we met an elderly couple named Grant and Jean, whom we had seen at the local Episcopal Church in Glasgow, Virginia. They invited us for dinner, both before our New York trip and again afterward.

As we were chatting during the second evening, I looked at Grant and suddenly realized, from the side, he looks exactly like my father—and I mean exactly! The resemblance in profile was uncanny, but not from the front! I had not recognized any similarity the first time I saw him.

I checked with Jamie on the way home, and apparently, he had seen the likeness between Grant and my father when we first met them.

When I finally became aware of Grant's uncanny similarity to my father, I became sure it was the cue to my flashback. It's just like psychologist Christine Courtois noted that a flashback "... usually occurs in response to some *stimulus* [emphasis added] in the present environment."[66] And therapist E. Sue Blume significantly adds that "Many times flashbacks [are caused by] ... a person who has similar characteristics [to] the perpetrator."[67]

When I finally recognized the connection between Grant and my flashback, I still felt a heavy load of pain and evil. It was discouraging. I also sensed all the turbulent emotions I had buried when I was unable to handle them as an eleven-year-old.

I became aware of the fact that just talking through the abuse in psychotherapy—which I had done for years— was not a protection from flashbacks. Dr. van der Kolk pointed out our higher brain has two sides. The left side is the factual one you tap in talk therapy. The right side stores memories of sound, touch, smell, and, most importantly, the emotions; it cannot easily be accessed by talking.[68] The flashback came from the right side of my brain, not the side that responds to talking.

On the train I had apparently gotten stuck as an eleven-year-old because the right side of my brain with its sensory overload was making me relive the abuse experience all over again. The cure would be to get myself back to my current age, where I belong. I was trying to do it by writing poetry and extensive journaling, but any improvement was slow.

A strange dream I had at the time appeared to have brightened my mood noticeably. In the dream, Jamie and my father were both masturbating in front of me. I was distressed. I told them they were disgusting, and I removed myself from them. When I awoke, I realized that I, in some manner, had put a limit to their abusive behavior, not literally, but by removing myself from their presence.

I don't remember my father ever masturbating in my presence, but I've concluded the dream might have reflected a prior reality. The presence of Jamie established the time element. He was old enough to be sexually competent, but we weren't married. Within the timeframe, I was still living at home with my father and experiencing the shower incidents. Second, I felt terror, anger, and disgust in the dream—the same emotions I experienced during my flashback. I assumed they were feelings that originated during the abuse itself. The third—and most important—element was that I felt noticeably better since the dream. I established a boundary in the dream, and now some of the suffering and terror were lifted.

I eventually realized my father could have been masturbating while he was watching me shower during my senior year. I pretty much kept my eyes closed while bathing so I wouldn't have to look at him. He only pulled a tiny portion of the shower curtain back in order to see me. Most of his body was hidden behind the curtain. Assuming he was masturbating, I would very likely not have noticed. I was engulfed in my own world of embarrassment, shame, and anger. But even if my father didn't do the act in front of me, the dream still carried emotional weight and truth.

A final clue to the flashback was that I must have dissociated when I saw Grant the first night, which means I had a sudden, temporary lapse in conscious awareness. The dissociation was due to my conscious mind failing—or refusing—to recognize Grant's similarity to my father. If my conscious mind *had* allowed me to see the similarity between my dad and Grant the first time, I probably would not have had the flashback.

The researcher Judith Herman believes a child victim may develop a "contaminated, stigmatized identity" from the abuse because she takes the "evil of the abuser into herself."[69] I clearly felt a sense of evil during the flashback.

After this experience, I believed the feelings from the abuse could never blindside me again. Experiencing them during the flashback, therefore, was important for my peace of mind. Being in touch with the emotional aspect of the abuse represented another type of closure, I think, measured by my believing the abuse had finally lost its power over me!

23

RESEARCH NOTES
DEEP WOUNDING:
MEMORIES RESURFACE

As I was writing this book, I discovered Jamie's and my understanding and acceptance of my affair had remained unresolved, even after many years. He put away his intense feelings, allowing us to get on with the business of salvaging our marriage. Jamie and my agreement worked well for many years, but his negative feelings had recently re-surfaced.

Every March he and I go away for a few days to mark the anniversary of Jeffrey's death. On the way home about five years ago, Jamie told me he had been having thoughts and vivid dreams about my affair with Jack. It was all he said at the time. I remember learning that flashbacks come without warning and take one back in time. For Jamie, the flashback took him back to the night of my affair some fifty years ago.

Over the next few weeks, Jamie became very angry and more and more anguished. He had a difficult time sleeping because his dreams were of the affair.

I found it difficult to face the consequences after this much time had elapsed, but I believed it was simply more collateral damage from my initial abuse. Although I had grown in many ways, I felt we both needed to resolve the affair.

We hadn't figured out the cue for Jamie's flashback, but we both noticed it started while our niece Jobi was battling brain cancer. I had been visiting her frequently; visiting was difficult, time-consuming, and expensive. I'm afraid I concentrated on Jobi too much when I was with her, which would have been fine if Jamie had not been in the middle of a crisis. He wondered if he felt neglected and abandoned by me when I visited Jobi—and if this could have been the trigger for his flashback. It, at least, could have been a contributing factor.

Trying to handle both Jobi's serious illness and Jamie's anguished flashback was terribly difficult. I tried to be responsive and solicitous to Jamie as he worked through his feelings. At the same time, I offered love and support to Jobi and her family, who had been going through their very difficult ordeal. It was tremendously hard. Both situations were immensely painful for me. I was unhappy, anxious, and depressed.

I felt very guilty for Jamie's anguish but not really able to help him. He was furious with me. Fortunately, he understood he needed outside help. Signing on to psychotherapy was good for him and for us.

I had a hard time with Jamie's anger when he lashed out at me. A friend warned me not to become defensive, but I found it extremely difficult not to. I knew he had every right to be angry, but the affair was many years ago. As I noted before, Jamie repressed his anger for years.

I realized I hadn't been much help to Jamie. Nothing I offered him as an explanation was satisfactory. In all candor, I still found my behavior back then really difficult to understand. I was well aware that my action seriously threatened our marriage. I tried to be reassuring about my deep regret, but Jamie wasn't in a place where he could hear me. I honestly didn't know what to do.

For Jamie the pain from his memories was progressing unabated for some time. He shared with me a quote he found on the Internet. He told me it described how he felt at the time very well:

"The betrayal that infidelity represents is a profoundly hostile act that permanently alters relationships whether or not reconciliation and

'forgiveness' allows them to continue. If the choice is to reconstitute the marriage, both people live with the knowledge that, whatever they meant when they promised their love and imagined that their hearts would be safe with the chosen other, that person intentionally hurt them in the most profound way. This is more than a violation of a promise ('forsaking all others')"[70]

It is a very powerful statement, which makes me feel terrible. I didn't know how to make it up to Jamie. Perhaps I could not undo the damage, but I hoped we could work at building something new—and stronger—together.

At this point, I was both weary and fighting depression. But I finally found a way to use words to help explain my previous actions, and they seemed to reach Jamie. It went back to my drive for self-actualization, an idea which seduced me. The idea, frequently espoused by Jack, was what drew me to him, not a romantic or sexual attraction. It seemed to make sense to Jamie, as it did to me. I can remember myself well enough back then to know the idea would have been very appealing to me.

We had been talking a great deal about the concept, which evidently resonated with Jamie. I could see he had begun to feel better, and I thought I would conduct a search on the Internet to see what I could find out about the causes of infidelity. I discovered I could have been affected by several different motives or influences. Only a few of them mentioned sexual abuse as a causal factor [see below], but there were many other reasons for adultery that were not directly related to sexual abuse or did not apply to me.

One interesting study was conducted by psychologists Marc Whisman and Douglas Snyder. They found, in their work with married American women, "... that a history of forced sex during childhood was associated with an increased risk for sexual infidelity, compared with those reporting no history of forced sex."[71]

A Canadian study reported in 2016 provided support for this conclusion. The prevalence of extra-marital affairs for child sexual abuse survivors were … "more than twice as high as those observed in non-victims."[72] And family psychologist, Shirley Glass, notes that "men and women who were sexually abused during childhood or adolescence may engage in compulsive sexual behaviors as a consequence of the earlier trauma."[73] Wendy Maltz, a sex relationship therapist, indicates that survivors may show certain symptoms either immediately or years later, which may include 'compulsive or inappropriate sexual behaviors.'"[74]

Several studies show a link between early sexual experiences (assuming the possibility of sexual abuse) and affairs. In a *Redbook Report: A Study of Female Sexuality*, the results of a survey of 100,000 women revealed that extramarital sex by 48% of women whose first sexual experience occurred at age fifteen or younger [mine occurred at age eleven], was in contrast with only 16% of women whose first sexual experience occurred after age twenty-one. [75]

A powerful statement was made by researchers Gerald Faria and Nancy Belohlavek, who noted, "Survivors may tend to sexualize all relationships;"[76] their statement was reiterated by Kathleen Ratican[77] several years later. Sue Blume might agree, noting that when the survivor "… feels attracted to another person, she may define the attraction as sexual." This is in place of all the other possible levels of interest she may feel, like "… the desire for understanding, or nurturing intellectual stimulation, or excitement over shared interests … all of these … she tends to reduce and misdefine as sexual."[78]

A website called *The Female Stage of Infidelity* provides another clue to my inexplicable behavior. The site states that "the reason many women give for their desire to separate (from their husbands) is to 'search for self.'"[79]

And then there is Esther Perel, a well-known couple's therapist, who observes that "we have affairs not because we are looking for another person, but because we are looking for another version of ourselves. It's not our partner we seek to leave … it's ourselves."[80]

The loss of self spoke to me, even after all these years. Erikson notes that during the ages from eleven to thirteen [when I was abused] the teenager ... begins to form the self, which is defined as a sense of one-self and "that distinguishes [oneself] ... from all others."[81] And Cole and Putnam add that incest may cause deviations in the "... processes of defining, regulating, and integrating aspects of the self..."[82] For me, the process was interrupted, making me wonder whether I was looking for a self during the affair.

It reminds me of something I read in Susan Harter's book: "... clients with dissociation identity disorder [such as I exhibited] ... represent the self as a disjointed collection of autonomous agents [or parts], but often ... different ego states will be in diametric conflict with each other. For example, a sexually promiscuous [ego state] will be countered by another, morally upstanding personality ... ."[83]

Perhaps I had two different ego states at war with each other, which is how the infidelity happened.

There appeared to be other external factors not related to the abuse, possibly playing a role in my infidelity. For example, there is evidence that friends can influence one to practice adultery. Jamie and I have wondered about it because we were such good friends with Vicki and Jack, who had an open marriage.

I remember reading a quote from Dr. Lynne Atwater, who interviewed, in great depth, some 50 women engaged in extramarital relationships. She observes that "knowing a person who had already had [an affair]" is often a significant factor in pursuing this course, especially the first time. "About one half of the women knew such a person ... these 'role models' were friends." Nearly all of the women interviewed said that "they had no thought of becoming involved [in an affair] at the time of their marriages."[84] It was also true of me.

Another factor, which may have influenced me, was the idea of patterns developing in families of origin and affecting later, adult behavior. It may occur if the adult is unaware of the possibility of repeating behavior observed in childhood.

According to my mother, for instance, my father often visited a prostitute in Utica, New York. The question, therefore, was whether my father's behavior with extramarital sex set up an unconscious potential pattern of acceptability in my brain.

There is a reference from clinical psychologist Ana Nogales, which supports the idea. She notes that "… 55% of adult children, who came from families where one parent is unfaithful, ended up being cheaters themselves."[85] Add to the fact here that the cheating parent in my case was the same parent who sexually abused me, and it would seem as though the cards were stacked against me.

Jamie's feelings about my affair, while difficult for me as the perpetrator of the infidelity, opened the subject up for many long-overdue discussions between us. It was an intense process, but we pursued the issue until we reached some explanations, which made sense to us both. Slowly, our conversations headed toward reparation and renewal. We gained an increased understanding of my aberrant behavior. It felt like we have been healing a very old wound.

I was extremely grateful for Jamie's work in trying to understand where I was coming from, and, ultimately, for his forgiveness. In our early years together, I often took Jamie for granted. I realized recently how often he was my champion. Jamie accepts me, loves and respects me, and has taught me that two people can live together in harmony. He stood by me and was always a source of love and care for me and our children.

Throughout our marriage, I had many underlying issues and many demons dancing around inside me, which pushed me to act against my own, and Jamie's and my, self-interest. Neither of us understood my compulsions at times, and we had no idea how to address them. I am very glad he stuck by me through it all, and now, with a little more clarity, he and I can talk, heal, and move forward.

I know I have healed in many ways, and Jamie has also. Of course it has been a great benefit to our relationship—and it gives me great confidence we have learned the skills we might need to handle whatever lies ahead.

AFTERWORD

I t has taken me six years to write my story; I learned more and more about my behavior as I progressed, as there was a great deal I did not understand.

I have finally finished writing after numerous re-writes and professional editing. While mine is the story of one survivor, it is a symbol for many survivors. May all our voices be raised in honor of us survivors, who have risen above our past and are celebrating our new-found freedom.

As you read my story, I was sexually abused at the age of eleven by my father. At the time, I put the abuse away as best I could, but I was unknowingly acting out for years because of the trauma. I have described my unhealthy behavior in my story; it continued until my sixteen-year-old son committed suicide. Unexpected, I was devastated. I was worried about my survival and sought help from both my minister and a female psychotherapist I saw for counseling. She helped me forgive my son, and she was only the second person to whom I told the full story of the abuse. Telling these stories was an enormous relief to me.

There the matter stood ... until I started writing my story. This caused me to look at my behavior much more critically than I had done before, and I found myself wanting to understand the things I had done. Why did I stop eating when I got to college? Why did I have an affair despite the fact I loved my husband dearly?

Faced with these difficult questions, I began doing my own extensive research, where I learned how many of these unhealthy behaviors are described in the literature because they are linked to the sexual abuse. Suddenly I had answers to my questions as to why I had behaved as I did.

My book became a vehicle by which I finally was able to understand my aberrant behavior. I hope it will promote a better understanding for you of your journey from your past to a brighter future.

As I mentioned earlier, I have finally discovered the abuse has lost its power. It has been over 60 years since it happened, and I have done a great deal of work on the issue. I had never been able to forgive my father, or grieve for him, because I was angry. But I realize now the anger has finally dissipated. I have no idea how or why this has happened, but I do not need to know. I can simply accept it as a gift, and it has allowed me to be free. And with this freedom, I found that I had forgiven my father. I have no doubt he loved me; our early interaction demonstrates it, but he made some very poor choices as I matured.

ENDNOTES

1 CDC Reference: https://www.cdc.gov/violenceprevention/childabuse-andneglect/childsexualabuse.html

2 Bessel van der Kolk, *The Body Keeps the Score* (New York: Viking, 2014) p. 306.

3 Ibid., p. 211.

4 Erin Carpenter, *Life, Reinvented: A Guide to Healing from Sexual Trauma for Survivors and Loved Ones* (Denver: Quantum Publ. Group, 2014), p. 36.

5 Riki Thompson, "Trauma and the Rhetoric of Recovery: A Discourse Analysis of the Virtual Healing Journals of Child Sexual Abuse Survivors," in *Journal of Composition Theory – Special Issue, Part 2: Trauma and Rhetoric, Vol. 24*, No. 3, (JAC, 2004), p. 653–677.

6 Karen Duncan, *Healing from the Trauma of Childhood Sexual Abuse*, (Praeger Publishers, Westport CT., 2004), p. 3.

7 Donna S. Martsolf, and Claire Burke Draucker, "The Legacy of Childhood Sexual Abuse and Family Adversity," in *Journal of Nursing Scholarships, Vol. 40*, No. 3, 2008, p. 335.

8 Duncan, op. cit., p. 58-60.

9 Rachel Devlin, "Acting out the Oedipal Wish: Father-Daughter Incest and the Sexuality of Adolescent Girls in the United States," 1941–1965, *Journal of Social History, Vol. 38, Issue 3*, (2005) p. 609. (Citation to Judith Herman, *Father-Daughter Incest*, Harvard, 2000.)

10 Karin C. Meiselman, *Incest: A Psychological Study of Causes and Effects with Treatment Recommendations*, (San Francisco: Jossey-Bass Publishers, 1978), p. 116.

11 Ibid. p. 151.

12 David Finkelhor and Angela Browne, "The Traumatic Impact of Child Sexual Abuse: A Conceptualization," *American Journal of Orthopsychiatry, Vol. 55, Issue 4*, doi: 10.1111/j.1939-0025.1985.tb02703.x, 1985.

13 Carolyn Spring, https://www.carolynspring.com/blog/powerlessness, Jan. 2011.

14 Thomas Jefferson quote, May 31, 1791.

15 Vocabulary.com Dictionary.

16 Denise J. Gelinas, "The Persisting Negative Effects of Incest," *Psychiatry, Vol. 46, Issue 4,* 1983, p. 319.

17 Bessel van der Kolk, op. cit., p. 129.

18 Carolyn Ainscough, and Kay Toon, *Surviving Childhood Sexual Abuse,* (London: Fisher Books, 2000).

19 David Finkelhor and Angela Browne, op. cit., p. 532.

20 Bessel van der Kolk, op. cit., p. 21.

21 Robert L. Barker, *Social Work Dictionary,* (Silver Spring, MD: NASW Press, 1991).

22 Mary Ann Cohen, *French Toast for Breakfast: Declaring Peace with Emotional Eating,* (CA: Gurze Books, Carlsbad, 1995), p. 62.

23 L. Rice, R. C. Hall, P. T. Beresford, P. J. Quinones, and A. K. Hall, "Sexual Abuse in Patients with Eating Disorders," *Psychiatric Med. 7(4),* 1989 p. 257.

24 Stephen A, Wonderlich, Ross D. Crosby, J. Mitchell, K. Thompson, Jennifer Redlin, G. Demuth, and J. Smyth, "Pathways Mediating Sexual Abuse and Eating Disturbance in Children," *International Journal of Eating Disorders, Vol. 29,* 2001, p. 27.

25 Cohen, op. cit., p. 62.

26 Ibid., p. xiv.

27 Ibid., p. 18.

28 Ibid., p. xv, p. 53.

29 Ibid., p. 75.

30 Ainscough and Toon, op. cit.

31 Cohen, op. cit., p. 62.

32 Hilda Bruch, *The Golden Cage,* (Cambridge, MA: Harvard University Press, 1978), p 59.

33 Ibid., p. x.

34 Ibid., p. 77.

35 Bessel van der Kolk, Alexander McFarlane, and Lars Weisaeth, Editors, *Traumatic Stress, The Effects of Overwhelming Experience on Mind, Body, and Society*, (New York City: The Guilford Press, 1996), p. 190.

36 E. Sue Blume, *Secret Survivors: Uncovering Incest and Its Aftereffects in Women*, (Hoboken, NJ: John Wiley and Sons, 1990), p. 50.

37 Judith Herman, M.D., *Trauma and Recovery: The Aftermath of Violence— from Domestic Abuse to Political Terror*, (New York: Basic Books, Harper Collins, 1992), p. 60.

38 Bessel van der Kolk, "Terror, Trauma, and the Sacred: Psychological, Clinical, and Religious Perspectives"—The 2014 Merle Jordan Conference, (Boston: The Albert and Jessie Danielsen Institute, 2014), www.bu.edu/danielsen/conferences/2014-jordan-conference.

39 Christine A. Courtois, *Healing the Incest Wound: Adult Survivors in Therapy*, (New York: W.W. Norton and Co., 1988), p. 98.

40 Duncan, op. cit., p. 38.

41 Some of the studies showing a link between depression and child sexual abuse are: Joseph Beitchman, Kenneth J. E. Zucker, Jane E. Hood, Granville A. da Costa, Donna Akman, and Erika Cassavia, "A Review of the Long-Term Effects of Child Sexual Abuse. Child Abuse and Neglect," 1992, pp. 106–107. Debra A. Neumann, Beth M. Houskamp, Vicki E. Pollock, and John Briere, "The Long-Term Sequelae of Childhood Sexual Abuse in Women: A Meta-Analytic Review," *Child Maltreat*, 1, 1996, p. 6, 13. Elizabeth O. Paolucci, Mark L. Genuis, and Claudio Violato, "A Meta-Analysis of the Published Research on the Effects of Child Sexual Abuse," *Journal of Psychology*, 135, 200, p. 17, 26. M. A. Polusny and V. M. Follette, "Long-Term Correlates of Child Sexual Abuse: Theory and Review of the Empirical Literature," *Applied Preventive Psychology*, Vol. 4, 1995, p. 145-147.

42 Melissa Hall and Joshua Hall, "The Long-Term Effects of Childhood Sexual Abuse: Counseling Implications," Retrieved from http://counselingoutfitters.com/vistas/vistas11/Article_19.pdf., 2011, p. 2.

43 Ellen McGrath, "Child Abuse and Depression," *Psychology Today*, May 2003.

44   Kathleen A. Kendall-Tackett, Linda Meyer Williams, and David Finkelhor, "Impact of Sexual Abuse on Children: A Review and Synthesis of Recent Empirical Studies," *Psychological Bulletin, Vol. 113, Issue 1,* 1993, p. 164.

45   Valerie E. Wiffen, Janice M. Thompson, and Jennifer A. Aube, "Mediators of the link between childhood sexual abuse and adult depressive symptoms," *J. Interpersonal Violence,* 15 (10), 2000, p. 1100.

46   Duncan, op. cit., p. 38.

47   Medical Daily, https://www.medicaldaily.com/effects-child-sexual-abuse-depression-and-other-mental-health-conditions-247591.

48   Mauro Garcia-Toro, Jose M. Rubio, Margalida Gili, Roca Miguel, Chelsea Jin, J. Shang-min Liu, Camilla Bastianoni, and Carlos Blanco, "Persistence of chronic major depression: A national prospective study," *J. Affective Disorders, ttp://dx.doi.org/10.1016/,* 2013, p. 3.

49   M. Hartman, S. Finn, and G. Leon, "Sexual-Abuse Experiences in a Clinical Population: Comparisons of Familial and Nonfamilial Abuse," *Psychotherapy: Theory, Research, Practice, Training,* 24, 1987, p. 154–159. (Cited in Hall and Hall, op. cit.)

50   L. L. Long, J. A. Burnett, and R.V. Thomas, "Sexuality Counseling: An Integrative Approach," (Upper Saddle River, NJ, Pearson, 2006). (Cited in Hall and Hall, op. cit.)

51   Kathleen L. Ratican, "Sexual Abuse Survivors: Identifying Symptoms and Special Treatment Considerations," *Journal of Counseling Development, Vol. 71,* 1992, p. 33–34.

52   Duncan, op. cit., p. 105.

53   Ibid., p. 62.

54   Tony Bates, *Foreword by Paul Gilbert, Understanding and Overcoming Depression: A Common Sense Approach,* (Berkeley, CA: Crossing Press, 2000), p. 16.

55   Pamela M. Cole and Frank W. Putnam, "Effect of Incest on Self and Social Functioning: A Developmental Psychopathology Perspective," *J. Consulting Clinical Psychology,* 60(2), 1992, p. 174–184.

56   John N. Briere and Diana M. Elliot, "Immediate and Long-Term Impacts of Child Sexual Abuse," *Future Child, Vol. 4, Issue 2,* Summer/Fall, 1994, p. 54–69.

57   Bessel van der Kolk, *The Body Keeps the Score: Brain, Mind, and Body in the Healing of Trauma,* (NY: Viking, 2014) pp. 62–63.

58   Beverly Engel, "Facing the Pain of Child Abuse," https://www.psychology today.com/us/blog/the-compassion-chronicles/201802/facing-the-pain-child-abuse.

59   Courtois, op. cit., p. 98.

60   Eileen Kennedy-Moore, "Suicide in children—What every parent must know," *Psychology Today,* Sept. 24, 2016.

61   Tom Whitehead, "Boundaries and Psychotherapy, Part 1: Boundary Distortion and Its Consequences," Hakomi Forum (on-line). Available: http://goodandwell. com/survivor/bound1. Html, 1993, p. 7–16.

62   Erin Carpenter, op. cit., p. 50.

63   Duncan, op. cit., p. 47.

64   Wendy Maltz, *The Sexual Healing Journey: A guide for Survivors of Sexual Abuse,* Third edition, (NY: William Morrow, 2012), p. 143.

65   Bessel van der Kolk, op. cit., p. 198.

66   Courtois, op. cit., p. 300.

67   Blume, op. cit., p. 103.

68   Bessel van der Kolk, op. cit., p. 47.

69   Herman, op. cit., p. 105.

70   M. D. Livingston, and S. Gordon, "Infidelity and intimacy," https://www.psychologytoday.com/us/blog/lifelines//infidelity-and-intimacy, 2011.

71   Mark A. Whisman, and Douglas K. Snyder, "Sexual Infidelity in a National Survey of American Women: Differences in Prevalence and Correlates as a Function of Method of Assessment," *Journal of Family Psychology,* 21(2), 2007, p. 152.

72 Marie-Pier Villancourt-Morel, Caroline Dugal, Rebecca Poirier Stewart, Natacha Godbout, Stephanie Sabourin, Yvan Lussier, and John Briere, "Extradyadic Sexual Involvement and Sexual Compulsivity in Male and Female Sexual Abuse Survivors," *Journal of Sex Research*, 33(40), 2016, p. 621.

73 Shirley Glass, Not *"Just Friends": Rebuilding Trust and Recovering Your Sanity After Infidelity* (NY: Free Press, 2004), p. 268.

74 Wendy Maltz, "Sexual Healing from Sexual Abuse," *SIECUS Report 29.1*, Oct/Nov, 2000, pp. 17-23.

75 Robert J. Levin and Amy Levin, "The Redbook Report: A Study of Female Sexuality," Reprinted from June, September and October 1975 issues of *Redbook Magazine*, (CO: Redbook Publ. Co., 1975).

76 Gerald Faria and Nancy Belohlavek, "Treating Female Adult Survivors of Childhood Incest," *Social Casework*, 65(8), 1984, p. 465–471.

77 Ratican, op. cit., p. 34.

78 Blume, op. cit., p. 216.

79 Women's Infidelity, "Why Women Cheat and Have Affairs," womensinfidelity.com.

80 Polly Veran, "Is Anyone Faithful Anymore? Infidelity in the 21st Century," *The Guardian/The Observer*, March 6, 2010.

81 Barker, op. cit., p. 210.

82 Cole and Putnam, op. cit., p. 4.

83 Susan Harter, *The Construction of the Self: A Developmental Perspective* (The Guilford Press, NY, 1999), p. 274.

84 Lynn Atwater, *The Extramarital Connection—Sex, Intimacy, and Identity* (NY: Irvington Publishers, 1982), p. 30, 60.

85 Anna Nogales, Ph.D., *Parents Who Cheat: How Children Are Affected When Their Parents Are Unfaithful*, https://www.thedailybeast.com/how-infidelity-affects-kids, July 13, 2017.